"This powerful book will touch your heart and change the way you want to live. In an era of digital convenience and social networking, people have rediscovered a yearning for meaning in their life and work. They want real connections and true human contact. Starting in the Ninth Ward of New Orleans before Katrina, Jane and Scott Wolfe built a business based on those values. To walk into their place today is amazing: it's a restaurant, laundromat, book salon, children's reading zone, and all-round community center. Kids who bring in report cards with an 'A' get a free cake and their parents get a free po-boy sandwich. This book chronicles their amazing journey and their vision that could serve as a model for every neighborhood—and every entrepreneur—trying to recapture the joy and love that comes from true community."

—Walter Isaacson, author, historian, journalist

"We all live lives of sometimes-congruent, sometimes-clashing intersections—of our experiences and acquaintances, our ambitions and disappointments—but the story that Jane and Scott Wolfe tell here of their myriad intersections in New Orleans is a uniquely inspiring one.

It combines region, class, race, gender, hard work, and growing faith in ways that should help any reader open his or her heart to the possibilities of good that exists in all of us. Most importantly, it tells of how we can take what is inside us and translate it into tangible, lasting accomplishments that lift up and give back to the lives of so many around us, if only we learn how to act on what is inside us all.

Against extraordinary odds, this couple built not just a thriving series of businesses but gradually a culture of service and community we should seek in our own lives to emulate. I was one of Jane's Harvard professors and so can vouch for the authenticity of what she and Scott describe here. Read, learn, and remake yourself by taking in and then acting on their experience and lessons in your own life."

—Professor Richard Parker,
Harvard Kennedy School of Government

"I don't think I have ever heard a more inspiring story of how, via social entrepreneurship, Jane and Scott Wolfe built not one but several businesses. The Wolfes' account of their journey is one of those rare works that is at once a thrilling page-turner but also chock-full of important lessons for all of us who have or want to take the road less traveled in business and life. It is unflinching in its description of the sacrifices required and the rich rewards reaped along the way. Each time, they achieved astounding financial success while embodying the kinds of values that enrich our lives and make this world a better place."

—Rupert Scofield, president & CEO of FINCA International,
author of *The Social Entrepreneur's Handbook*

"Scott and Jane Wolfe's journey epitomizes the values of perseverance, passion, and a commitment to community. As they have traveled on the road to business success, they have kept the community and people that are their customers front and center and, as such, have defined what it means to function as a double bottom-line business in twenty-first-century New Orleans."

—Marc Morial, mayor of New Orleans (1994–2002)

"This book is an inspiring must-read for anyone looking to grow a business. The Wolfes share their secrets for success, building customer relationships even as they work to build and improve their community. They prove that being good corporate citizens isn't a trade-off you make with profitability; it is instead the driver of success."

—Devin Thorpe, author and Forbes contributor on social entrepreneurship and impact investing

FROM GED

TO HARVARD

THEN INC. 500

FROM GED

HOW TWO TEENS WENT FROM GEDS TO BUILDING

TO HARVARD

THE FASTEST GROWING BUSINESS IN NEW ORLEANS

THEN INC. 500

JANE & SCOTT WOLFE

ForbesBooks

Published by ForbesBooks, Charleston, South Carolina.
Member of Advantage Media Group.

ForbesBooks is a registered trademark, and the ForbesBooks colophon is a trademark of Forbes Media, LLC.

Printed in the United States of America.

10 9 8 7 6 5 4 3 2 1

ISBN: 978-1-94663-337-8
LCCN: 2020902384

Cover design by Carly Blake.
Layout design by David Taylor.

This publication is designed to provide accurate and authoritative information in regard to the subject matter covered. It is sold with the understanding that the publisher is not engaged in rendering legal, accounting, or other professional services. If legal advice or other expert assistance is required, the services of a competent professional person should be sought.

Advantage Media Group is proud to be a part of the Tree Neutral® program. Tree Neutral offsets the number of trees consumed in the production and printing of this book by taking proactive steps such as planting trees in direct proportion to the number of trees used to print books. To learn more about Tree Neutral, please visit **www.treeneutral.com**.

Since 1917, the Forbes mission has remained constant. Global Champions of Entrepreneurial Capitalism. ForbesBooks exists to further that aim by bringing the Stories, Passion, and Knowledge of top thought leaders to the forefront. ForbesBooks brings you The Best in Business. To be considered for publication, please visit **www.forbesbooks.com**.

To our parents. They loved us first.
To Scotty and Jennifer. Y'all make life beautiful.
To Jude, Claire, Luke, Nora, and Ollie. Y'all make life fully alive.

CONTENTS

ACKNOWLEDGMENTS

Our deep gratitude goes to Gertie, Bucket, Sherrill, Tom, Leonard, Michael, Freeman, Andrew, Lois, Edwin, and Keith. In those days before Hurricane Katrina, your hearts filled our hearts. Thanks for making Wagner's Meat the best it could be for every single person in the Ninth Ward. This book could not have been written without y'all.

Reading through the text, you'll notice magnifying glass symbols (as seen above) placed at key areas. When you see this icon, you can refer to the QR code section at the back of the book. These QR codes will direct you to further resources on the subject matter.

WHAT'S DESIRE GOT TO DO WITH IT?

Successful businesses speak to peoples' souls, fill their hearts, and invite them to be part of something greater.

Your customer can buy that widget or that sandwich or that pedicure anywhere. Your employee can get a job to pay the bills anywhere. What they really want, without really knowing it, is meaning.

Our society is looking down the barrel of an instant gratification epidemic. We no longer need to walk outside for a conversation, to go to work, or to even buy groceries. If we want it, it's ours with a click—no human interaction required.

But that's simply not how we're designed to live. We need each other. We need meaning and purpose. We need support. We need our communities to look on us and say, "We like you, and you are valuable to us."

And this all starts with a desire to look at each other in the eyes.

That is why we were able to do what we did.

SHOTGUN

SCOTT»

It sounds strange to prepare for a robbery.

It was Mr. Roosevelt, a loyal customer, who told me about it, shaking the sleet off of his coat as he shambled in at 10:00 a.m. He found me in one of the store's narrow aisles, stocking shelves.

"Be careful," he said, his voice low. "I heard some dudes at the bus stop say they gonna rob you."

There were only three of us in the store that day: Pam, the cashier; Jane, sixteen years old and seven months pregnant, at the meat counter; and me, the seventeen-year-old store manager. I wasn't sure if Mr. Roosevelt was telling the truth or just trying to get a free pint of Night Train out of me for the tip, but it wouldn't hurt to be prepared.

I didn't tell Jane or Pam what I was doing or why. I just took the majority of the cash out of the register and hid it in the back-office filing cabinet. I also tucked a .38-caliber gun in my waistband, hiding it with my shirttails, and folded a .22 pistol under my arm. I wasn't nervous. I thought I was ready.

Customers trickled in and out of the store that morning, sparse in the unseasonably cold weather. An hour passed and nothing happened. I was starting to relax a little. Maybe Roosevelt had been pulling my leg. Should've never given him that wine …

Suddenly a figure swept past me wearing a raincoat and hood. He kept his head down as he walked purposefully toward the back of the store. I followed him, pressing the pistol to my chest and feeling the weight of the .38 against the small of my back. He walked right up to the meat counter—a six-foot-tall antique behemoth that was all steel, porcelain, and glass—and slipped behind it.

I couldn't see what he was doing. All I could think was, *Oh my God, he just went behind the meat counter.*

Jane didn't scream as he pulled her out with him, gun barrel pressed to her temple. She just looked at me, eyes wide, terrified. I held her gaze, willing her to believe that it was going to be okay, that I would take care of this.

But I didn't know what I was going to do. I was going in circles with that one thought, wondering what to say, what to do with the guns. Then Jane looked over my shoulder and gasped. Suddenly an arm latched around my neck and I felt the cold press of gun metal against my neck.

"Get on the ground," a voice said.

Just then I remembered that I still had the .22 under my arm … and it was pointed directly at the guy's chest behind me. I hesitated. Should I pull the trigger? Would the small bullet do the trick?

I was taking too long. The robber's gun pressed even harder against my neck.

"On the ground!"

I didn't shoot. Instead, I slowly put one hand on the ground, and with the other I slid the .22 between the buttons of my shirt and lay down on top of it. That decision would give me nightmares for months afterward.

Once down, the second guy fleeced me and found the .38. Before I knew it, he was jerking me up by my collar, and the .22 fell out, clattering on the tile. He picked it up without a word. I glanced at Jane and saw the surprise on her face. She didn't know I had a gun on me, let alone two.

"Back of the store," said the first guy. "Show me where you keep the money."

This time, I didn't hesitate. I took them right to the cash I'd hidden earlier. There was no point keeping it from them. Again, they forced us onto the ground and told us not to look up.

"Did you hide any more?" the second guy demanded. "This better be all there is. You better tell us the truth, because if we find more, we gonna kill you."

We heard them rip open the rest of the filing cabinet drawers, going through everything, threatening to kill us if they found more money.

KNOW TRUTH

JANE »

Even though he'd taken the time to hide it earlier, Scott didn't hesitate to tell the robbers exactly where the money was. He told them the truth even before the robbers demanded it.

I can still hear them shouting, "You better tell us the truth!" over and over again.

In truth, these kids *had* to rob us. They were living in deplorable conditions, and they had nothing and no way—in their minds—of getting out of those dire circumstances. They knew the "truth" of what was right and wrong, moral and immoral, and yet they robbed us because they had no money. They were balancing truths. They had to take to live.

SCOTT »

I didn't look up. I didn't want to. All I could think about was how much it would hurt, waiting for the sound

> All I could think about was how much it would hurt, waiting for the sound of gunfire, wondering if I'd hear it before my head exploded.

of gunfire, wondering if I'd hear it before my head exploded. Time stopped.

Then there were customers shaking us, telling us it was okay, we could get up.

No, I thought. I can't get up. They told us to stay down.

The feeling was akin to when your leg goes numb and you have to wait until all the pins and needles are gone before you can walk on it. Finally we got up and realized that they were gone. We were alive.

It was like a baptism.

❖ ❖ ❖

TWO KIDS WITH GEDS

JANE »

Eighteen years after the **Civil Rights Act** passed, we—a couple of white kids barely out of our teens—started a business on **Desire Street** in the heart of New Orleans's Ninth Ward.

We had grown up in Chalmette, an average-size city just southeast of New Orleans on the banks of the Mississippi River. Our families were both entrepreneurial. Scott's father ran a construction business, and my father opened a grocery store when I was in middle school. My mother, too, ran her own business, and it was thanks to her that an entrepreneurial flame burned strong and true in my heart. They were, and still are, incredibly hard workers and they were our inspirations.

SCOTT »

There's no peace in a house with five brothers.

I was anxious to get out of that 1,200 square feet of chaos. Getting married and moving out at the age of seventeen was a welcomed relief but still scary and uncertain. A chance to finally make my own path.

I never really knew my oldest brother, Tommy, that well. He was lost to drug addiction by the time I was ten, casting a shadow on our house that never quite faded away. Too young to really understand any nuances about Tommy and his impact on the family, some impressions burned into me forever. I wouldn't ever touch drugs. I grew heart for hard circumstances. And for my family on the fringe, I wanted to serve as a counterbalance.

My brothers Michael and Keith surprised me. As much as I was determined to be on my own when I left home, they became a part of our lives in such a way that Wagner's and later Melba's wouldn't have been possible without them. Early on, it was my brother Mike who made it possible for Jane and me to purchase the very first Wagner's Meat. Later, it was Keith who made it possible for us to open a new Wagner's location, and after Hurricane Katrina ripped through, took the reins on running the day-to-day operations at Melba's.

As for my other brother, David ... I'll tell you about him in a minute.

A TEN-YEAR-OLD'S CONTRACT

SCOTT»

My family taught me a lot. Even though it was another lesson in my young life about what *not* to do, it was my dad who taught me about the importance of organization, opportunity, and risk.

My dad was a general contractor and started tagging me along to job sites when I was about ten years old. We'd see my older brothers working there with the tradesmen, but I'd go sit in on the breakfast and lunch meetings, listening to him make deals for new jobs.

Those meetings were what shaped me into a businessman.

I learned the banter, the expressions, the "tells" that meant someone was on the verge of being sold … or about to walk out the door. I learned how to negotiate and how to find opportunity in unexpected places. And I learned what *not* to do.

My dad's methods were a mess. If he bothered to create *any* paperwork, it would be a mess too. Nothing was written down; he just kept it all in his head. I tried to help him organize it all once by typing up new contracts and making homemade ledgers for estimating jobs, but he just patted me on the head, said they looked good,

11

and never used them.

He was the last of the old-school business types, working in what they called "big bullseyes." He would just ballpark a number, and the customers would accept it as the professional cost. There was no internet, no comparison shopping, no online ratings or reviews to consider. Back then, competition had borders, and technology was a working calculator plugged into an electrical outlet. Even then, however, I understood how important it was to do the best work possible, to exceed customer expectations, and to learn a craft so well you could do it in your sleep. People may pay you to do a job the first time, but they're not going to pay you a second or third time if your first work is crap.

> I understood how important it was to do the best work possible, to exceed customer expectations, and to learn a craft so well you could do it in your sleep.

❖ ❖ ❖

IMPERFECTION HAS CONSEQUENCES

JANE »

"Grocer" was actually my father's second career. For more than thirty years before he bought **Ideal Food Store,** three blocks from the **Desire Housing Project,** he clocked in and out at Kirschman's, a local furniture store. During the week he sold furniture and carpet, and on the weekend, with Mr. Kirschman's permission, he cut doors for customers so they would fit with the new carpet.

It was my dad who taught me the importance of details and taking your kids to work.

I remember being about ten years old when I went with him on those weekend jobs. He was always cutting these heavy, massive doors in tall New Orleans mansions, taking careful measurements, gingerly removing the hinges, and placing the doors on stands so he could trim the bottoms in perfectly straight lines.

"If the door is too long, it'll scrape the carpet fibers," he explained to me. "If that happens, the carpet will look worn well before its time. Imperfection has consequences, Jane. Details are everything."

Then he'd reinstall the door, test it to make sure the swing was perfect, and meticulously clean up after himself before leaving. For two years I went on those weekend jobs with him, and we never got a single complaint.

THERE'S AN ENTREPRENEUR IN ALL OF US

JANE »

Mom also worked weekends, cutting hair for the local ladies. She set up one of the rooms in our house as a salon, and Dad built an outside entrance to it with a hand-carved sign above the doorway that read "Joy's Beauty Salon."

Although it was the way in which Dad ran Ideal Food Store that shaped my understanding of business, it was my mom's beauty shop that first introduced me to entrepreneurship. Seeing her successfully run a business gave me confidence that I could do the same. Mom was the one who taught me the importance of sticking with what you start and always giving your customers more than they expect.

> Mom was the one who taught me the importance of sticking with what you start and always giving your customers more than they expect.

My mom's business experience and my dad's obsession with detail were a prelude to their grocer days. Once they purchased that modest

15

neighborhood corner store, they were behind those counters every day, making certain every item on the shelves was rotated, that the labels faced forward, and that every po-boy was perfectly toasted and overstuffed with meat.

Because of where it was located, the neighborhood probably would have settled for less than the meticulously clean, reliable store we offered the community, but because our family worked so hard to make Ideal an enjoyable place to visit, the neighbors appreciated it and loyally shopped with us. And when the people of the neighborhood we served worked with us, they were loyal and engaged employees.

I did not finish high school. Once my pregnancy became obvious, my Catholic school forced me to drop out. Still, my shortened education was light-years ahead of New Orleans's public school system, which helped later on when—twenty-eight years removed from the classroom and with only a GED in hand—I attended Tulane University, graduated *cum laude* with dual degrees in history and religious studies, and followed up with Harvard Divinity School, where I graduated in 2015 with a masters in theological studies. Today, I teach a course simply titled World Religions.

Through it all, from our **shotgun marriage** to building a multimillion-dollar grocery chain in New Orleans's inner city and to losing it all in Hurricane Katrina and rebuilding once again, we were, and continue to be, extraordinarily lucky.

New Lives ...

JANE »

Our wedding day was a celebration of love and family. Aunts, uncles, cousins, grandparents, brothers, and sisters all danced together, and before we knew it, we were out of our tux and gown and on the road toward our honeymoon destination. Where would a fifteen- and a seventeen-year-old want to go for their honeymoon? **Disney World,** 🔍 of course!

We drove down the lonely stretch of state highway through Alabama and into the Florida Panhandle until we were so tired, we could barely see. Finally we found a motel with a vacancy and caught a few hours of sleep before hitting the road again.

Disney World was amazing, more for the fact that we were entirely on our own than for the amusement park itself. We had no curfew and no one we had to answer to. If we wanted to go on a ride more than once, we just looped back around and got in line again. For three days we were like little kids, enjoying every last moment of our newfound freedom.

On the way back we drove straight through, avoiding a motel stay to save money. When we got home, we went to Scott's parents' house first...and his life, for the second time in three days, changed forever.

... And Life Lost

SCOTT »

Before the car pulled into the driveway, my brother Keith was running out of the house, his face pale.

"He's dead," he said as I got out of the car. "David's dead. Motorcycle accident."

It was as though I'd stepped into a tunnel, one that emptied into my house and into my living room, where I passed by my family members as though they were statues. I could barely hear them asking me if I was okay and couldn't hear my father sobbing on the sofa, even though I remember thinking that until that moment, I'd never seen him cry. I watched myself silently glide past him until I was in the kitchen, looking at Mom. When she saw me, she, too, erupted into tears.

I felt like I should cry, and I might have. I don't remember. Time had stopped, and the universe had taken a very tangible left turn. It had never really occurred to me that the people I loved deeply could be taken from me so quickly, without notice. Three days before, David had been the best man at my wedding. Now he was a ghost. I would never speak to him again, never meet his future wife or see his children grow up. I would never know who he would become. Why? How was that fair?

That surreal feeling stuck with me over the next few days. We got ready for the funeral and had lunch afterward, where everyone kept eating because they didn't know what else to do. It still gives me chills to think about it. Sudden death is difficult to accept when it happens to people who have lived their lives. When it happens to the young, the pain is somehow sharper.

After David's funeral, I tried to live by a new rule: treat every moment with loved ones as though it is the last time we'll meet, because we all know how it ends … we just don't know when.

IDEAL SITUATION

SCOTT »

It wasn't long after Jane and I started dating that her father, Johnny, decided to purchase the old Ideal Food Store. Since he knew I had a strong work ethic from a short time we had worked together at the furniture store, he asked me to come work for him. I agreed immediately, not just because it meant being closer to Jane, but because I knew how Johnny operated. He had excellent business smarts, and I knew he wouldn't just show me *what* to do in the grocery business—he would show me *how* to do it and *why*.

Jane and I worked at Ideal Food Store sixty-five hours a week, scrupulously saving, absorbing the business process, and keeping our eyes on the future. We knew we didn't have a lot then but were determined to find a way forward.

❖ ❖ ❖

THERE'S A CHANCE HERE

JANE »

By all accounts, we should not have succeeded.

We were teenagers with a child, opening a small neighborhood grocery in the heart of New Orleans's most solid black community. The infamous Ninth Ward had some of the nation's most challenging drug, crime, and poverty problems as it struggled with the burden of a pervasive prison mentality brought on by unlivable housing, deplorable infrastructure, desperation, and a government that had temporarily lost its bearings.

We didn't have much to start with, but comparably, our struggles were profoundly naïve. Our education was cut short by a teenage pregnancy and a shotgun wedding but was light-years ahead of the education that left the kids in this neighborhood unable to even read and write. Our families saw drug addiction and death, but it wasn't the kind of suffocating loss that seeped in through every nook of life as it was sometimes in this neighborhood. Our parents taught us and showed us important lessons about business, work, entrepreneurship, and hope, but many in this neighborhood never got those lessons.

Saddled by our own youth, struggle, and busy calendar, we didn't notice how much even this separated us from the community's plight. Sometimes, we still don't. And we made mistakes.

Our neighbors could have turned against us, treating us as effigies of a system that cared less about them than it did its own crumbling drainage system.

But they didn't.

We saw the personal and systemic battles our neighbors dealt with every day and grew an intense respect for the neighbors we served. The community here was surviving. Through the years, our family spent a lot of our waking hours together.

We shared a smile together when customers came into Wagner's, and our neighbors would often take time to ask about our young children and chat about the day.

It's easy to categorize and blame and debate something in the abstract. *Those* people. *That* neighborhood. To *fear* the other environment or what the other environment can do to you.

But in a local grocery store, it's *that* person right there with their two eyes. There is constant face-to-face interaction.

In establishing the Jesuit Order, Ignatius Loyola commanded in the *Constitutions of the Society of Jesus* to "employ all possible love, modesty, and charity" so that environments could flourish in "greater love than fear."[1]

We aren't perfect. We aren't Jesuits. And we didn't start out with any intelligent design whatsoever in how to reconcile the moat between us and the Ninth Ward neighborhood. But we were in the thick of it all and face-to-face with this community, and to some material degree, we started there with more love than fear.

People could feel that we cared about their needs and their

---

1   Constitutions of the Society of Jesus, #667.

families, and that we truly wanted to interact and talk. This is one of the deepest needs of the human condition: the desire to engage. As useful as technology has become, we all still crave that personal interaction, to be seen and acknowledged, to share a smile with another human being, and to not simply be just silent cogs in the wheel of society.

So we racked our brains to find ways to convey the unspoken love and respect we held for the neighborhood that we served.

An old-style "readerboard" at front of our store was an early example of this, a tiny square of white plastic that I started filling with messages of hope, changing the words every day. The board could have said something as simple as "God is Love," and yet the joy it brought to our customers was profound. We could have used the readerboards to drive sales—something Scott originally favored—but we increasingly used it to spread messages and good news to the neighborhood. After twenty years our signs became neighborhood landmarks that people would go out of their way to see.

Over the years, our customers discovered that we cared. We offered an impeccably clean store to shop in, we greeted every person who walked in the door with a genuine welcome, we had a butcher who knew everyone's name and favorite cut of meat, and in our hearts, we kept the inner fire of respect burning.

I can't say for certain that this is why our stores flourished, but I believed it helped. We didn't start with assumptions. Instead, we opened ourselves up, thanking our fellow man for giving us the chance to make something of ourselves, and in return, we gave the neighborhood the opportunity to do the same.

In Judaism, the highest form of giving[2] is providing someone a job. In our heart of hearts, every human being wants to be needed,

---

2   Known as *tzedakah*, the moral obligation to do what is just and right.

to feel capable, and we did everything we could to make this gift possible. We hired our neighbors, offering jobs based solely on quality of character. If the candidate showed up to the interview on time, brought the documents we requested, and dressed respectfully, we tossed their handwritten resume without a glance and told our new employee when to show up for the first shift.

On occasion, convicted felons were some of our best employees. People who never knew how to read or use a calculator learned on the job and excelled. Others, who never knew what it was like to be given opportunity at work, went on to have careers and even started their own businesses. For so many of our employees, **we were the first ones outside the home** 🔍 to ever say, "You really can do whatever you set your mind to."

We did everything we could to make our jobs fit our employees' needs. We purposefully scheduled overtime for those who wanted it so that they didn't have to hold down two or three jobs to survive …

But I'm getting ahead of myself. Scott and I will talk about this more later on. For now, I simply want you to understand that it takes thinking about these kinds of things (what will help the single working mothers, the marginalized and hard-working men, and all others in between) to build what we built—a ten-store, multimillion-dollar business in one of the most historically poverty-stricken areas of the United States—and to come back from the destruction of those businesses to start the fastest growing company in Louisiana.

Many people are not privy to the conditions in which Scott and I, and our businesses, came up. We learned from our circumstances and spent hours each day thinking about how we could make things better for those who touched our lives every day: our customers, our staff, our neighbors. We wanted the neighborhood to know that they had a chance here, that this was not all that life could be. And we honored that message by giving the neighborhood we served the best that we could give, whether that was a sparkling clean store to shop in or a free ice cream cone for hard-earned school grades.

We didn't have a name for what we did back then, but today you might call it "engaged entrepreneurship" or "corporate social responsibility." *Everyone* is in the service industry, and those who have a true and deep respect for each other—those who radiate that unspoken factor—are those who can survive anything. Just as we did *with only* **GEDs**. 🔲

Not Too Far from Ideal

JANE »

For a few years both before and after we got married, Scott and I worked at my father's store, an old-fashioned neighborhood grocery called Ideal Food Store.

It was small, maybe a thousand square feet in all, with three aisles so full of groceries that the stack from one would block the fluorescent light from spilling into the next. We worked hard to keep that store meticulously clean and well stocked, and we prided ourselves on our customer service.

And the neighborhood appreciated us for that. We had loyal shoppers, and the people who worked for us were just as loyal and engaged. Roosevelt was one of those loyal customers, and when he heard some kids down at the bus stop talking about how they were going to rob our store, he came in and told us immediately.

It took me decades to realize that the young man who had held the cold barrel of a gun to my forehead was compelled into his situation by a universe of motivations that I could never understand. Whatever those circumstances were, they led that kid—not much older than I was at fifteen years old—to stop just short of pulling the trigger and ending my life.

I was lucky: lucky to have a courageous boyfriend, lucky to have had fifteen years of a stable and loving home life before that day, and lucky to have that humble little store fill my head with business knowledge and ambition.

> We live in a challenging world. It's on us to decide whether we'll be the victor or the victim.

That kid who disappeared from our store with a wad of cash, sweaty palms, and a racing heart? I'm pretty sure he and I had very different lives.

I'd like to speak to that young man one day—though he's not so young now, of course, some forty-plus years after the robbery—and find out what drove him to rob us and what kept him from shooting us. There must have been something in him that was directing him. Was it the words of his grandmother or mother? Someone in his family who struggled to teach him right from wrong? In my heart, I know that people are not born to do evil. Sometimes they find themselves with few options and opportunities, but even criminals would rather have a better life. We live in a challenging world. It's on us to decide whether we'll be the victor or the victim.

I strongly believe in the power of community and that education, love, and support (or lack thereof) ultimately guide our decisions, which is why I want to talk with him about his life, his childhood before he walked in our store, that contributed to life in Angola prison.

I want to know why he didn't kill us.

SCOTT »

I was haunted for months by dreams of that **robbery.** 🔍

Every night, the story took a different twist. Some nights I was

Clint Eastwood, shooting the robbers and saving the day. Other nights we were both killed. More often than not, I woke up in the middle of the dream sweating, gasping, not knowing that night's outcome and not wanting to know.

JANE »

Apart from turning a profit, security became Scott's highest priority from that day on. He needed to know his customers and employees were safe, that they wouldn't have to go through what we did. And his family. Through the years, his brothers, my sisters, their children, and our children all worked with us, spending countless hours roaming the aisles.

And it wasn't as though we could turn to the police. In the 1980s, when we started out, there were a lot of rogue cops in New Orleans. When a place got robbed, it was most likely an inside deal. Security cameras became the only truth, and we relied on them to tell it. A couple of decades later, one little Kodak camera actually ended up saving Scott $120,000. But Scott will tell you more about that later.

SCOTT »

It was in those sleepless hours that I decided I would never be in such a vulnerable position again. I didn't just want my wife and I to be safe. I wanted to own stores where everyone was safe—customers and staff.

Several times over the next two years after the robbery, Jane and I scoped out grocery stores for sale. Of the ones we could afford, most showed little promise and were in very poor condition. Then a meat supplier told me about a small bankrupt grocery named Wagner's that wasn't too far from Ideal.

We checked it out that evening. The store was in bad shape: dark, dingy, and with almost no inventory. The present owner, Charlie, did his best to paint a rosy picture of the place, but even my optimistic young mind saw a very steep hill to climb.

It was Tom, the butcher, who finally convinced me to buy it.

Tom was a wise man, not in the way of formal education, but through life. I knew at once that there was a lot he could teach me, and I was hungry to learn. In fact, I've found through most of my life that some of the most talented and knowledgeable among us don't necessarily come from a background of formal education.

> Some of the most talented and knowledgeable among us don't necessarily come from a background of formal education.

Wagner's was Tom's first and only employer. He'd started there when he was twelve years old, working for the founder, T-Boy Wagner, until **T-Boy was shot and killed by his wife.** 🔍 The son, not wanting anything to do with the grocery business, sold it to Charlie, a retired New Orleans police officer with poor spending habits.

"Charlie's not a businessman," Tom told me once Charlie was out of earshot. "He don't restock, and he only wanna buy new cars."

"Before Charlie," said Tom, smiling as he reminisced, "it was a whole other world."

In the same way we'd remember a lost love, Tom described the meat counter line that used to stretch out the door and down the street. Wagner's Meat had such a reputation for quality back then that people would sometimes wait hours for their cuts of meat. With the right person behind it, Tom said, this store could turn around.

That was all I needed to hear. Wagner's was a gamble I was willing to make. All we needed to do now was scrape together $20,000 to buy the place.

Unquenchable Curiosity

JANE »

For a long time after we opened Wagner's, we debated on whether to keep cutting fresh meat or to switch to packaging, but a good butcher is a rare find. They are the stars of neighborhood grocery stores, remembering how regular customers like their deli meats sliced, saving specific cuts for different folks, and trimming the bone and fat exactly the way people like. That was what Tom—a slender, unassuming man about twenty-five years our senior—did at Wagner's. He'd spent a lifetime perfecting his skill, and he wielded his blades like a master craftsman. Which he most certainly was.

When we met, Tom couldn't read the newspaper, but he constantly had the radio in the back of the butcher shop tuned to the news. Talking with him was the highlight of my day for a long time. He was constantly teaching me about the grocery and meat business. Like my father, he was a stickler for details, and while he may not have had a lot of formal education, he was one of the wisest men I'd ever met.

I'll always remember the day he taught me about the Interstate Highway System. Every year, Tom and his wife took their homemade camper van somewhere in the United States. I'd been around the country myself, but I'd never really thought about the numbers assigned to the interstates until Tom explained them to me. His face lit up as he pointed out how the even numbers indicated traveling east to west, and the odd numbers were for roads traveling north to south.

It was a simple fact, but it was fascinating. I'd never had the curiosity to wonder about the numbering of Interstates, but Tom's curiosity was unquenchable. He had so much knowledge, and he was so excited to share it with us. For the next twenty-five years, Tom was a major part of our team. We wouldn't have been Wagner's Meat without Tom … a truth neither Scott nor I really understood until Hurricane Katrina brought it all crashing down. In losing everything, we finally realized all that we had had and how much more we could have done for our Wagner's family. We should have done more.

Sometimes, you get a second chance.

INTEREST, PLUS A CADILLAC

SCOTT»

The thing was, about a month before we found out about Wagner's, Jane and I had spent our life savings, a whopping $10,000, on a brand-new 1982 Crown Victoria, purchased straight off the sales floor from Bill Watson Ford.

Hat in hand, I went to see Mr. Watson in person and begged him to return my money and finance the car. Even though he said he would consider it, he eventually turned us down, which meant I had to start making the rounds to family and friends.

My first stop was Uncle Buddy. He'd retired from an oil refinery years ago and seemed to have the finer things in life, like a nice home, new cars, and a built-in swimming pool. He wasn't a blood relative, but he was such a close friend that we considered him family.

I tried to hide the full reason for my visit when I asked to see him. Aunt Jeanette met me at the door and walked me to his home office, announcing in that gently booming voice of hers, "Scottie's here!"

Uncle Buddy was sitting at his desk when I walked in. He was a big, quiet man with bushy eyebrows that peeked over the top of his glasses.

"What can I do for you?" he asked.

Rushed, I told him about the grocery and its potential and asked to borrow the money we needed to purchase it.

The next questions Uncle Buddy put to me were as tough as a bank interview, each one unraveling my fantastic opportunity until all I was left with was a flimsy, high-risk idea. I could see him slipping away from me, so in desperation I promised him a high interest rate "and a brand-new Cadillac."

I smiled, thinking, Who could turn that down?

> A deal that sounds too good to be true will drive people away, and overpromising will lead to suspicion and disbelief rather than trust.

But Buddy's eyebrows rose even higher than they'd been before, and he slowly shook his head.

"I'm sorry, Scottie," he said, "but my monies are all tied up in my pension."

"I understand," I said, trying not to show my disappointment. "Thank you for your time."

Even though I didn't get the money, Uncle Buddy held a mirror up to my presentation, which helped me pivot for the next dozen pitches. I needed to make the offer reasonable. A deal that sounds too good to be true will drive people away, and overpromising will lead to suspicion and disbelief rather than trust. The car, I learned, was too much. It diluted my ask and made me sound desperate. I'd do better on the next try.

DREAM TO DO WELL

SCOTT»

I couldn't shake the thought of Wagner's. I daydreamed about it at work, picturing how I would turn it around, imagining the lines of customers once again stretching around the corner like they did in Tom's rose-colored memories.

JANE»

To do good things, we need to imagine them first. Scott believed so strongly in owning Wagner's, he actually pictured himself doing it. Concretely imagining it in a *creative visualization* like an athlete may visualize the plays of a game. And this prepared us for the famous "luck is when opportunity meets preparation" phenomenon, driving Scott and me to make owning a business a reality.

SCOTT»

One day, out of the blue, a guy named Mike walked into Ideal. He'd been a loyal customer at the store for years, but this time, he wasn't in to buy groceries.

"I hear you're looking for a partner?" he said, smiling.

Mike was a bail bondsman with an easygoing personality. When he said that, I almost leaped out of my shoes.

"Yes!" I said and proceeded to tell him all about this failing store and what it would take to turn it around. Something I said must have hit home because despite the hurdles I had described, he said he was in. Ten thousand dollars for a fifty-fifty partnership.

Now all we had to do was scrape together our half.

Somehow, word that I was going around to family members and asking for money got around faster than I did. It felt like everyone knew what I wanted even before I opened my mouth, but I still tried. Each and every one of them seemed prepared with an excuse: don't have it, money is tied up, just made a big purchase, etc. But that didn't deter me. Perseverance is a virtue that has gotten me through just about every challenge and opportunity I've encountered in life. *Never give up*, I told myself, and I never did.

> Perseverance is a virtue that has gotten me through just about every challenge and opportunity I've encountered in life.

I was running out of relatives to ask when my brother Michael gave me an unexpected lead. His friend Mark, who owned a restaurant and who's family ran a successful coffee import business in town, wanted to see me.

I dropped everything and went straight to Mark's house.

Of all the people I'd told about Wagner's, Mark interrogated me the least. When I finished my pitch, he simply picked up a brown paper bag that was sitting on the table next to him and tossed it to me, telling me to pay him back when I could.

I opened the bag. It was all there, $10,000 in cash. No interest, no sharing a piece of the business, no contract, not even a Cadillac. Just, "Pay it back when you can."

I ran home to find Jane sitting on our bed. Instead of telling her what had happened, I just opened the bag and threw the money around her on the bedspread. She was shocked.

"How?" she asked, and I told her about Michael and Mark and the unbelievable loan. We held each other and laughed, rolling on the scattered bills and thinking about how our lives were about to change.

Scomik, Inc.

SCOTT»

Mike the bail bondsman and I purchased Wagner's Meat under the name Scomik, Inc., short for Scott and Mike. A few days later we were up and running. Fortunately, I already had a relationship with most of the vendors from my days at Ideal, so I was able to get the store stocked on credit—and stock it we did. We packed all 1,500 square feet of that little space to the gills.

Two weeks later, the daily sales had doubled from $200 to $400. It still wasn't enough to pay the bills, but we were getting there. We worked from 6:00 a.m. to 7:00 p.m. every day, Jane at the cash register, our son in the playpen next to her, Mike and I on the floor, and Tom, our only employee, at the meat counter. After we closed, Jane, Mike, and I would often stay until 9:00 or later doing renovations, painting, and stocking.

Best Years Given to Work

JANE »

Every single day, my mind was geared toward three things: business, kids, and family. My husband lost me to work, but he was okay with that. He was gone too.

But what I didn't realize, what I didn't appreciate at the time, was that there are only 200 months available to be a mother. My mind was always on sales, marketing, and grocery orders. It was never "off" so that I could appreciate those special, tender years as a mother.

I will never forget one summer day when I watched from our kitchen window as our son Scotty played basketball with some neighborhood friends. At twelve years old, he was the youngest one on the court, but he was holding his own, and I was proud of him. After a while his friends left, and Scott, still full of energy, came running into the house, basketball tucked under his arm.

"Mom, can you come out and play a game of Around the World with me?" he asked, sweat dripping from his handsome, still-boyish face.

My response to him still haunts me.

"I don't have time for basketball," I said. "I have to clean up and make a grocery order."

I would give anything to go back to a simple, ordinary day like this one and start over with what I know now. I would have run outside and played basketball with my son in a heartbeat. That grocery order could have waited!

I have little memories of simply holding to appreciate a sleeping child in my arms or enjoying a room full of laughing children because I was always multitasking, always trying to think of the next thing we needed to accomplish with the business.

A mother should never place any business over her greatest job of all time. I was quite lucky because this was our business.

SCOTT»

It wasn't long after we opened our doors that we got our first shoplifter. I saw him slip a Twinkie into his coat pocket and try to slip out the door.

That was not going to stand.

I immediately leaped over the counter and ran after him. Mike, not knowing what was going on, jumped up and started running after me. The pursuit lasted several blocks, me chasing the shoplifter and Mike chasing me, until the three of us crossed Desire Street and the shoplifter cut behind a liquor store into a wooded area. I kept on after him, but Mike stopped at the tree line and went back to the store.

"Scott is crazy," he told Jane when he got back. "He just ran into a wooded area for no reason at all."

A short time later I came back, proudly holding the stolen Twinkie. Mike just shook his head, more shocked than amused.

That day turned out to be one of the longest yet. By the time we closed the doors, we still had seventy-five cases of product that needed to be priced and rotated, all the boxes needed to be broken down, and the store still needed to be cleaned.

Mike was exhausted. He wasn't used to the long hours, and it was showing.

Sensing opportunity, Jane suddenly pounced.

"Hey, Mike," she said. "You want out of the grocery business? We'll pay you double your investment in six months."

Mike's eyes went wide, and he turned to me.

"Scott, did you just hear what your wife said?"

I nodded. "If that's what she says, that's what we'll do."

Mike couldn't get his apron off fast enough. He laughed all the way to the door, acting for all the world like he'd just fleeced us.

> No matter what your pursuit, you have to give your efforts time to convert to results.

The next day was the best one we'd ever had. Sales hit $1,000 for the first time, and they never dropped below that line again.

Had our partner's fatigue not clouded his judgment, he probably would have decided against Jane's offer, but recognizing opportunity can go both directions. It was an important lesson in entrepreneurship for all of us: no matter what your pursuit, you have to give your efforts time to convert to results.

ACCIDENTALLY POSITIONED

SCOTT»

Everything in our market revolved around the meat.

Of the thousand square feet that made up our store, more than a quarter of it was the meat case: thirty-six feet of chicken, red meat, and "seasoning meat" (turkey necks and pickling tips), all expertly cut and displayed. Tom knew exactly what the customers liked, and if he didn't have what they wanted (which was rare), he introduced them to something else. Nine times out of ten, they took him on his word, and within a day or two they were back for more of the same. Tom was practically a celebrity, and while we may not have had lines for blocks of people waiting to buy cuts from him, we always had customers at the meat counter.

Yet we failed to see this as something unique.

❖ ❖ ❖

A HOUSE BUILT ON LUNCHEON MEAT

JANE »

We had an amazing butcher in Tom, but we didn't cater to the filet mignon market because those customers were so hard to please. Give me the hot sausage customer any day of the week! And that was just who we catered to. We knew what our customers wanted, and we gave it to them: pickle tips, pig tails, and ham seasoning for red beans and rice, crabs and sausage for filé gumbo, turkey necks and wings for a hearty stew, and in the summer, ribs, ribs, ribs, and leg quarters. In July, I saw leg quarters in my sleep.

These were the cuts of meat I had grown up with, the pickle meat and ham, liver cheese and luncheon meat. At Wagner's we sold thousands upon thousands of pounds of luncheon meat, buying it truckloads at a time, and even though we sold it dirt cheap, we still made a decent profit. We sold so much of it that I'm pretty sure our first home was built on luncheon meat profit.

SCOTT »

Sure, we had a great meat section, but my biggest concern was how we were going to get more people in the door.

For a while, we thought it was mailers. Twice a month, just like the big supermarkets did, we crafted a detailed sales flyer with produce and other staples at rock-bottom prices, hoping to get new customers in and to change up the shopping habits of our regulars. It worked for the most part, boosting that first triumphant thousand-dollars-a-day record to five-thousand-a-day and growing. But it was exhausting.

It wasn't as though we could simply pick a handful of items to put on sale that week. We had to lock in discounts with our suppliers months in advance, estimating how much we thought we could sell and then warehousing it until the sale. If we bought too much, we had to eat the loss. If we bought too little, the customers thought we'd lied just to get them in the store. It was the same thing every two weeks: Jane and I trying to balance on the razor's edge of too much or too little and endlessly chasing discounts on soda, milk, and bread, frustrated with the process but believing it was simply a necessary evil of the supermarket business.

Until one day when Jane picked up the book ***Positioning*** 🔍 by Al Ries and Jack Trout.

We read that book at least two times, straight through, and each page made more sense than the last.

"When you try to be everything, you wind up being nothing," Ries wrote. "The basic approach … is not to create something new and different, but to manipulate what's already up there in the mind, to retie the connections that already exist."

The realization hit me like a one-ton dollar sign. It wasn't about discounting potatoes to sell more stew meat or figuring out how to move three pallets of overstocked canned carrots in August. It was about lifting from where we stood, taking care of what was already in front of us. It was about being known for that One Thing we were already doing, and then doing all of our advertising around that.

But what would our One Thing be? Jane and I wracked our brains until one hilarious and purely unintentional comment from a customer gave us the answer.

❖ ❖ ❖

YOU CAN'T BEAT ...
WAGNER'S MEAT

SCOTT »

Tracy was one of our first and most loyal customers. She always had a smile for us and would often stop by just to chew the fat with Jane or me, and she had a respect for Tom that bordered on starstruck.

Then one day, Tracy came in with her sister in tow.

"Look at all of it!" 🔍 she said, almost dancing down the entire length of our meat counter and gesturing at the display like a game show model. Her sister giggled, but we could tell she was pleasantly surprised by the extent of our options.

"I told you," Tracy said, smiling. "You can't beat their meat!"

"Yup," I said from where I was standing with Tom behind the meat counter. "You can't beat our meat!" And we all laughed at the pun.

That line cracked me up the rest of the day. I must have said it dozens of times again that day, and each customer thought it was hilarious. When I got home, I told it again to Jane. We laughed, and right then I felt the same electric realization I'd felt after reading *Positioning*. That line, in all its pun-tastic glory, was the perfect motto for Wagner's, and I told Jane so.

Jane's smile quickly faded.

"What will the church groups think?" She frowned. "What about the families of small children?"

I shrugged.

"What will they think?" I said. "I don't know. But let's try it."

The very next day, I had our flyer artist draw up a new flyer with the Wagner's Meat logo as big as possible and our new motto underneath: "You can't beat ... Wagner's Meat."

❖ ❖ ❖

SEVEN WORDS OR LESS

JANE »

I didn't realize how deep the implications of our new catchphrase would be until we started hearing from the neighborhood associations. People didn't want our bright red-and-white slogan near their homes because of the innuendo. But that innuendo was exactly what made it so attention-grabbing! In marketing, the best slogans are dualistic. Just look at Coca-Cola's "It's the real thing," which implies that others might not be real. Without knowing it, we'd stumbled on a powerful line.

> The best marketing slogans, he said, are the ones that say everything about your business in seven words or less.

Later on, when **James Carville** interviewed me for his political science class at Tulane University, the first thing he said was, "You have to tell me who came up with that slogan. It's the best one I've ever seen!"

The best marketing slogans are the ones that say everything about your business in seven words or less, Carville said. Just look at the best marketing message ever written: "Love thy neighbor."

The whole of Christianity can be found in those three powerful words. It's remarkable how powerful just a few words can be.

SCOTT»

No one was more shocked than us by the results of that flyer.

Not one person came up to tell us how offended they were. Instead, our sales numbers began to grow ... and grow. We heard customers saying the motto to each other, more often than not with a twinkle in their eye and maybe even a wink, but it was catching on. Before long we'd trademarked the phrase, printed it on bumper stickers and T-shirts, and plastered it on our butcher paper. Sales skyrocketed, and we finally ditched the time-intensive mailer in favor of simple billboard advertising: no phone number, no location, no prices, simply, **"You Can't Beat ... Wagner's Meat."** Q

❖ ❖ ❖

THE WRESTLE

JANE »

Right in front of Wagner's was a small **readerboard** with just enough space for twenty short words. That little space became a source of serious contention.

Scott saw it as prime advertising space, the perfect spot for shouting about sales and getting people in the door. That's why the signs were first purchased, of course. When two-liter colas went on special for fifty-nine cents, he wanted the red numbers front and center on our *advertising* board.

I, on the other hand, saw an opportunity to do far more than open pocketbooks. In an area of deep poverty, I wanted to open minds. I knew we could engage with our customers on a much deeper level if, instead of marketing goods, we marketed good *news* instead.

So the wrestle began. We got in a lot of arguments about this in the first few years, and those early years saw a mixture of my messages and Scott's advertisements. Every time the board needed to be changed, Scott would pipe up. "Here we go again with Jane's quirky sayings … that do nothing!"

But I didn't let it stop me. I knew the power of words and the importance of being more than just a grocery store to our customers. If we could get these good thoughts out to the community, the community would associate good thoughts with Wagner's.

Little by little, the customers would come in and talk about the messages. People outside the neighborhood who *weren't* customers, those just driving by, would mention our readerboard messages in random conversations.

I knew we were having an impact when customers who couldn't read beyond a fifth-grade level came in and thanked us for putting this or that message on "the neighborhood board." It was a simple, openhearted act that brought smiles to people's faces and warmth to their souls.

Scott's passive dissent continued for quite some time, but I slowly accrued readerboard capital with him as the messages caught on. He eventually noticed that the messages actually helped his advertisements. At its peak, the readerboards across all our stores were seen by more than a hundred thousand motorists each day. And as people became regular readers, any ads we displayed got an attention boost.

This tension between Scott and me—his eye on the bottom line and my eye on the *double* bottom line—would have a mark on a lot of our arguments and a lot of our success.

ICE CREAM EMPATHY

JANE »

Our ice cream giveaway was another opportunity to do something benefiting the neighborhood (particularly the children) and our business.

During the school year, we put signs up letting parents and kids know that they got a free soft-serve ice cream cone when they showed us an A on their report card.

Over the years we gave out thousands of those cones, and at a cost of ten cents or so a cone, the return was exponential, not just in word-of-mouth promotion and customer loyalty but in the smiles it brought and the sense of accomplishment it gave. Children who heard gunshots in their neighborhoods came in with report card in hand and were instantly showered with praise.

Scott and I both have our memorable moments from the ice cream giveaway. Mine involves a little girl who came in with her mother. I wasn't at the ice cream station at the time, but I was nearby and overheard Michael, Scott's brother, review her report card.

Instead of smiling, however, Michael squinted at the paper and frowned.

"I'm sorry, but I can't give you an ice cream cone," he said. "This report card is all Fs."

The little girl's eyes filled with tears as her mother, shaking her head, marched up to Michael and turned over the card so that they could both see it. She scanned the paper and then pressed her finger on the very bottom of the page.

"Look here!" she said. "That's an A right there."

Michael looked and she was right. There was an A for good conduct.

When I heard the revelation of what the little girl's A was for, it startled my soul.

I'd met her several times before, and she was not only smart, she also had such a sweet disposition. Why wasn't her school working with her more to bring out the intelligence I could see burning behind those wide-open eyes? In an instant I felt the blow that politics and public policy had landed on the city's "urban experiment" school system. This child was innocent to the social catastrophe that was happening around her, and yet it was costing her every day.

I looked at the girl's mother, who smiled as Michael handed her the ice cream cone, swirled as high as he could get it without tipping over.

Thank God for the moms who fight for their children, I thought as the mother and daughter left, the little girl skipping between licks. *In the most trying of circumstances, that love and care can make all the difference in the world.*

SCOTT »

Jane always made sure our store was prepared for report card season. We stocked up on ice cream supplies and put the promotion on our billboards and readerboard (one of the few times she let us use that board for a store promotion).

Like the readerboard, it was something I didn't realize was working until we heard people talking about it. And not just a few people, either. People were *really* talking about it. Wherever we went—parties, schools, social events—people would come up to us and say what a nice thing the ice cream giveaway was. It was amazing how powerful that was. Even though only a small percentage of people took advantage of the offer, the word-of-mouth impact was huge.

It made it harder for me to argue with Jane when she came up with these kinds of ideas, the ones that reached out to the community and seemed to have no financial impact whatsoever. They might have taken a long time to simmer, but inevitably her outreach touched more people than a billboard or mailer could have.

When it came to the ice cream deal, there was one kid I'll always remember.

I was the closest one to the ice cream machine when the kid came in, report card in hand.

"Is this where we get the free ice cream?" he asked.

"Sure is," I said. "Is that your report card?"

He nodded and handed it to me, head down as though he was embarrassed.

Trusting the kid, I handed him his ice cream first, then looked at his report.

Just as I handed the cone over, I could see a look in the boy's eyes as though he didn't expect it, and for a minute, I couldn't understand why. The boy had almost straight As on his report card! But then I took a closer look. This was back in the days when report cards were handwritten, and as I looked at the letters, I could just make out where he'd drawn a line turning his Fs into As.

"You son of a gun!" I said.

The kid grinned as he walked away, licking his melting ice cream. I couldn't help but smile. *That boy*, I thought, *has one creative mind.*

Wagner's Meat Grows

SCOTT»

As Wagner's became more and more successful, I began to get "the itch." Our store had no room for growth, and parking was limited. Meanwhile, we were stockpiling cash, and none of it was "working" for us. We had to grow, so I started asking vendors what was for sale.

We began slowly at first, purchasing existing corner stores here and there as they became available and fit our specific needs.

There was Sclafani's Meat Market on Washington Avenue, Galvez Supermarket on Galvez Street, and Roots Grocery on Louisiana Avenue. We didn't change the names, just brought the Wagner's Meat approach to running them: clean stores, friendly staff, community-oriented promotions, and an excellent meat selection. We did well with them, and for a while, things were chugging along nicely.

Then one day I saw a closed car wash on North Claiborne Avenue for sale, and it struck me that all this time I was looking to *buy* the right store when what I needed to do was *build* one.

The highway was perfect. It was safer than the darker, less-busy side streets, which spoke directly to my deep-seated fear of robberies, and the car wash was in a prime location between neighborhood and commuter traffic. It only took a minute to call the guy on the sign, and in no time we were under contract for $150,000 owner financing.

Sweet Talker

SCOTT»

Our store on North Claiborne Avenue in the Lower Ninth Ward would become our first ground-up development, and our first bank-financed endeavor as well.

But it wasn't a quick or easy process. At first, not a single bank would have us. I didn't want to tap family resources if I didn't have to, but after the umpteenth bank rejection, I reached out to a bank co-owned by Dot Roper, a friend of my father-in-law. When she agreed to at least hear me out, I decided that the routine coat-and-tie office presentation wasn't enough. Dot needed more than just my words; she needed to see this place for herself.

I picked her up at the bank—still driving the Crown Victoria that almost lost us our chance at purchasing the first Wagner's—and drove her straight into the Ninth Ward.

We began driving through the backstreets surrounding the site, and I pointed out the sheer volume of homes and the number of people living in each, noting how few grocery competitors there were. In such an overpopulated, underrated part of town, there was vast potential for what we were doing … as well as enormous benefit to residents who, without our stores, were living in a "food desert."

Then I turned the car down a narrow strip of concrete with no houses along one side, just a steep embankment with a six-foot steel wall jammed into it like a long, straight set of false teeth. These were the levees, built to catch and siphon off flood waters in the event of a hurricane.

"This whole area is completely cut off from downtown New Orleans," I said. "There it is, on the other side of the bridge. But how are you supposed to cross that without a car? Even with one, even if you took the bus, why should you have to make that hike just to buy a loaf of bread or meat for dinner for your family?"

I swept my hand out toward the southwest and my hometown, the small precinct of Chalmette.

"And it's not that much better in the other direction," I told her.

"The lower Ninth Ward is a marketplace all on its own," I said. "It's starving in so many ways. You want statistical probabilities? You want reassurance that this is a good investment? Look around you. Have you ever seen a place in more need of a good, honest grocery store?"

Over lunch, I laid out our financial needs and sales projections. Then I answered her questions, and when she was done, we shook hands and she said she'd get back with me.

Days later, I got her answer. **Ms. Dot,** 🔍 the first woman appointed to The People's Bank board, would loan us $350,000.

It seemed like a million at the time.

❖ ❖ ❖

"WHAT DO YOU MEAN, 'CAN'T DO IT'?"

SCOTT»

It was family, once again, who came through for us on our first grocery build.

I spoke earlier about how I learned to be a businessman by listening to my dad make contracting deals. This time, it was me making the deal with him. We needed a store built from the ground up, and not just that, it was going to be our biggest store by far: four thousand square feet.

Jane and I poured every last bit of our experience and expertise into designing that building, from the entryway, to produce, to the best way to feature our namesake: the meat counter. Every day we were confident that this was the layout we wanted … and every other day we changed it. It drove my dad nuts, but it was our first time seeing a drawing translated from pencil and paper to an actual floor plan, so he did his best to walk us through it, and eventually we put down the eraser.

Some days it seemed like a hundred years and others only a

few days since we had first broken ground on the Claiborne project. Then, one day, it was ready. Construction was 99 percent done, and we were ready to start stocking the shelves. All we needed was the power company to come by and switch us to full power.

It only took a few minutes for the guy from the electric company to do a walkthrough. I saw him hitching up his pants as he walked over, flicking a chewed toothpick onto our clean tile floor as he said with a grunt, "Can't do it."

"What do you mean, "Can't do it?" I asked. "What is there to do? The power is running fine. We've checked it three times. Just flick the switch."

He shrugged. "Can't do it because you have the wrong equipment."

He walked over to one of our industrial meat cutters and pointed at the panel full of fine print and indecipherable warning signs.

"This here," he said, "is three-phase equipment. We don't have three-phase power in this area. So you plug this unit in, the best thing that could happen is nothing. It won't work. Worst case, you burn your new building down."

"Well why the hell didn't you tell me this before I built the place? How the hell am I supposed to know there are 'phases' of energy? I'm not a goddamned electrician!"

The engineer just shrugged again as though it wasn't his job to tell me anything.

"Okay," I said, trying not think about the tens of thousands of dollars of potentially useless equipment all around me. "Is there anything we can do to fix this?"

"Oh sure," he said. "Just buy a converter."

It is not that easy to "just buy" a three-to-single-phase energy converter. At least, it wasn't back then, before we could simply search for one on eBay or Amazon. Instead, we had to launch a nation-wide manhunt, turning over every stick and stone in the electrical equipment world to unearth what was, apparently, the last remaining phase converter in the world and priced to reflect that rare status: $3,500 that we didn't have. But we needed it, so we scrounged up the cash, bought it without knowing for certain whether or not it would work, and hooked it up.

Fortunately it worked well enough for the city engineer to deem our grocery store worthy of power. For the life of that store, it never stopped working, even though it remained red hot to the touch.

Accidentally Developed Convenience

SCOTT »

There's a special feeling lying in bed the day before opening a store. It's something only broke entrepreneurs feel after spending their life savings on one venture, working for months without pay on the desperate hope that their idea is going to work.

I must have stared at the popcorn ceiling above my bed for hours, praying for sleep and knowing it would never come.

Would even one customer show up? I wondered.

Why would someone who's never shopped with us before suddenly start buying from us?

Maybe this is all a huge mistake ...

It was a lonely and sobering drive to the store the next morning. The 6:00 a.m. traffic was sparse, and the fear-driven thoughts of the night before were starting to mingle with excitement. Whether or not a single customer walked in that door, whether they liked what they saw or if it was a complete failure from the start, we were about to find out. The moment was finally here.

It took closing the doors at the end of the day to finally stop the steady stream of customers from pouring in.

The funny thing was that this had just been a soft opening; there was no advertising driving people to our door, only word of mouth. We wanted to get all the kinks out before we announced our presence to the world, but it looked like the world had found us first. We were slammed—and we stayed that way day in and day out, with little ebb but lots of flow—and over time I came to realize that we'd stumbled on a new concept. By combining snacks, drinks, and quick meals with produce, dry goods, and our signature thirty-six feet of meat, we'd accidentally developed a convenience store within a neighborhood grocery store, and it was working like a dream. Finally, food was being sold in the desert.

A Shrimp-Based Land Purchasing Strategy

SCOTT»

After the success of the Claiborne location, I came up with a strategy for acquiring new land that was guaranteed to work every time. Before I decided to buy any new location, it had to satisfy eight benchmarks:

It had to have a "good feeling" about it.

It had to have strong vehicle traffic.

It had to have a significant number of surrounding rooftops.

It had to have that same "good feeling" six months later.

It had to be able to sell shrimp to motorists on site hand over fist from a pickup truck.

It had to fall within our mortgage appetite.

After drafting a sales-and-profit analysis for the location, Jane would always make me cut the estimate in half. If half worked, then it was a good location.

If I could convince Jane that it was a good location, I was ready to go to the bank.

Based on this strategy, I scoped our next location for a ground-up build: a lot in Central City at the corner of Martin Luther King Boulevard and South Claiborne Avenue. The spot still housed an empty Exxon gas station next to a row of abandoned shotgun houses, those narrow little homes that are only the width of one room with a door on either end. Exxon still owned the gas station, and the shotgun houses belonged to the owner of a pay-by-the-hour motel, who was happy to sell. All I needed was to have the city merge the lots into one large parcel and we could get to work on our new store.

It took some convincing to get Jane to realize the MLK location's worth. It was, after all, anchored in one of the highest crime and unemployment areas of the city. Literally, right across the street, some local church leased a billboard and simply displayed: "THOU SHALL NOT KILL." Once Jane believed in it, though, I knew I was ready to walk into any bank and ask for a loan. If Jane had confidence in it, the bankers were going to be an easy sell.

We began simply, with Scott Jr. and I going out to the lot and sitting in the open back hatch of the SUV, watching the red lights change.

"See all the cars going by?" I'd ask Scott Jr., who was about thirteen at the time. "See how they built so many curb cuts to this site? This spot is primed for action. It's busy, it's inviting traffic in and out. Can you feel it?"

After a while we'd hop back in the car, and I'd urge Scott Jr. to tell mom what he saw at the site and why he thought it was a good location. I knew I could almost never get Jane to go traffic watching with me, but Scott Jr. had a way of bringing her to my side.

It didn't take long before she was on board and talking to friends and family about our amazing new location as if she'd been in on it from day one. In 1994 we opened our second ground-up installation, and it did even better than the first. The process worked!

As long as there was land out there to buy, there was room to grow, and we were growing by leaps and bounds…until one day we ran head-first into a full-blown rumble with the City of New Orleans.

The Political Winds

SCOTT»

It all began as just another land purchase. I was fortunate to come across a gorgeous half city block of old **World War II apartment homes** in abysmal condition, and I bought the whole lot for just $1 million. It was perfect—a little narrow, but in a three-hundred-year-old city, you're not going to find many straight property lines.

The city wasn't going to just let me buy and develop that land without a little tête-à-tête. I needed permission for a beer-and-liquor license, so before the ink was even dry on the mortgage, I set up a dinner with the councilman who represented the district where the lot was located.

We met at the original Ruth's Chris Steak House on Broad Street, and over dinner I showed him the beautiful architect's renderings of a first-class Wagner's Meat, complete with a gas station.

He loved it, couldn't have been more supportive of the build, and as dinner wound down, he leaned back and said, "So what do you need from me? What can I do?"

"The only thing I need," I said, "is a beer-and-liquor license."

"That we can do," he said and smiled. "I can't wait to see that corner rejuvenated."

We were just getting up to leave when suddenly the city assessor walked by and noticed us.

"Scott!" he said, walking up with a ruddy grin and outstretched hand. "I heard you bought that old lot at the corner of 610?"

I nodded and shook his hand. The property was right on the corner of Elysian Fields and the I-610 interstate, what we called 610 for short.

"Well done, that lot is prime for rebuilding," he said. "Did you get the whole block?"

"No sir," I said. "Only the front half is zoned commercial."

The councilman jumped in. "Well don't let that stop you! Why, you buy it and I'll rezone it for you. You can't just go halfway on this—that whole corner could use your touch."

I smiled and thanked him for his support, and the very next day I had the property owner for the residential portion of the lot on the phone. We worked out a contract for the rear half of the property in record time, using most of my liquid cash to purchase it, and by that evening I'd signed the demolition permits.

It was only a few days later that I got an offer from a real estate agent interested in purchasing my newly acquired city block.

"Not interested," I said. "Land is hard enough to get around here, and this was not an easy purchase. But," I added, "everything has its price."

"In that case, let me talk to my client about making you an offer," he said.

We shook hands, and the very next day I received an offer from him: $1.2 million.

I laughed so hard I almost bruised a rib.

"Come on!" I said. "I've spent almost a year working on this project and invested one million dollars myself. I'd be lucky to clear $140,000 on this. Thanks but no thanks."

"In that case, good luck with your project," said the agent. "But my client isn't going to budge … and from what I understand, the political winds have changed."

Then he was gone.

I wasn't sure what he meant by that, but it gave me a very unwelcome chill.

It wasn't long before I found out either. Suddenly the rezoning process that the councilman had encouraged was inexplicably delayed. I would call city hall every few days about the permit's progress, and every time I was told "It's being processed."

Then the rumor mill began to churn. Almost every day I ran into someone who'd say, "What's going on with 610? I heard you're not getting the zoning," or "Tough luck with that zoning. What are you going to do with those Elysian Fields lots?"

For two weeks I called the councilman's office like a beggar, and all I got was silence. Finally, I decided to take matters into my own hands.

DOUBLE-CROSSED

SCOTT»

As chance would have it, the councilman was speaking at a private event a few days later, and it was only a matter of a few phone calls to get tickets.

I saw the look of surprise cross his face as our eyes met, and for the first half hour, the councilman shuffled around the room like an old girlfriend trying to avoid me. Enough was enough. I marched across the room and shook his hand.

"Councilman," I said and smiled. "How are you?"

"Fine, fine," he said, his eyes flicking around for an escape route.

"I've been trying to meet with you, but I can't seem to get you to call back," I said. "Is something wrong?"

He sighed.

"Come with me," he said, guiding me by the arm to a quiet corner of the room.

"Look," he said, running a hand down his face. "Here's the thing. I'd really rather something ... bigger ... happen with that corner. Why don't you just sell to those developers?"

That piddly little $1.2 million offer? I shook my head.

"Not gonna happen," I said.

"Well," he said, "then I can't support the project."

And just like that, he was gone, washed away in a crowd of supporters.

I knew right then that I had been double-crossed. Not only could I expect the zoning board to turn down my rezoning, I could kiss that beer-and-liquor license goodbye as well.

To make matters worse, the developers who initially approached me through the real estate agent continued to make offers—or, I should say, the same offer—every week, never budging on the $1.2 million.

They were waiting for me to cook, like cabbage on the stove. They knew they couldn't strike until I was soft, and if I was taking too long to soften, they just applied a little more heat. Eventually, they figured I'd break down. I knew. I'd used the trick a few times myself.

The developers kept putting more heat on the fire. They were making deals all over New Orleans for a Fortune 500 hardware store chain known for its bright, cool-tone box stores, and they had more lobbying money and political influence in one pinky finger than I could wield in a lifetime. I was boxed in, and their offer never wavered. The cabbage was almost cooked.

You Can't Beat Wagner's Meat ...

SCOTT»

We never did sell the land to those developers. And I never got the zoning I asked for ... or the alcohol license.

That **battle** ❑ turned out to be the opening shots in a never-ending war with New Orleans politics. Even as the public and bankers welcomed us with open arms, the politicians seethed and schemed. They weren't fond of a local businessman with twenty thousand customers per day whom they couldn't influence. I didn't need their favors, and that annoyed them, so they tried to boil the water under me.

Most often it began with a neighborhood group. In New Orleans, if you need something opposed, you pay a neighborhood group to come out against it. And the only way to get them to back off is to find who paid them, then pay them to "save" you. "Come-see-me" money is what they called it, and the only way to get around it was to hire politically connected architects and consultants, as well as our own neighborhood group, to support us.

"Necessary evils," they called it.

It made me furious until an old friend of mine made a very good point.

"Yeah, Scott, they f---ing you," he said. "But they not *really* f---ing you."

Even though I was paying out the nose in come-see-me donations, I was still catching a break. They were letting me build and operate my businesses, but if they wanted to—if they really wanted to—they could take everything I had.

❖ ❖ ❖

TROUBLEMAKERS ARE PRICE SENSITIVE

SCOTT »

As if the troublemakers outside our businesses weren't enough, the inside ones were keeping us on our toes.

It came as no surprise that we had shoplifters. Being in one of the highest crime areas of the United States, and with the memories of being held at gunpoint still firmly etched in our minds, security was always top of mind. But just like permitting, licensing and inventory wasn't easy.

Imagine for a moment running ten locations with nearly three hundred employees and serving about twenty thousand New Orleanians every day, twenty-four hours a day. It was the equivalent of running a small city. The phone rang around the clock—slips and falls, employee fights, stealing, audits, you name it. When you have regulators barging in unannounced with badges on their belts demanding to see this or that paperwork from five, ten, fifteen years ago, or visits from inspection departments without warning, a call about some minor shoplifting was almost a welcome relief. That was a problem we could solve. In fact, we figured out a way to get ahead of it.

It turns out that troublemakers are pretty price sensitive. They'll walk right by your store and go to a competitor for a one-cent price difference. So we upped our prices. Not a lot, and not on every-thing—just a few cents on the items that shoplifters were most likely to grab, like candy bars and beer.

Then we kicked it up a notch and tackled the items that trouble-makers were most likely to buy: we stopped putting wine on sale and got rid of Chore Boys—the wool-wire scrubbing pads commonly used for cooking crack—as well as rolling papers and cigars. And we upped all our beer prices by a quarter.

For a while, we were worried that the higher prices would drive away customers, but the fear was short lived. We not only recovered our sales, we grew right past them. Suddenly, we were the "premium store," and our competitors were merely discount locations. Our customers preferred the slight price increase because it meant that they didn't have to shop alongside the troublemakers.

That was possibly the single biggest "ah ha!" moment of my career. From that day forward, I constantly kept an eye out for products we could either get rid of or increase the price on in order to keep out questionable characters.

We were designing our customers, and we carried that concept into every store we opened from that point on.

The Right Hire

SCOTT »

Another way we curbed trouble at our stores was with our hiring practices. Not that I expected anyone we hired to rob us, but in just about every robbery I'd ever read about or witnessed, the thieves were somehow tied to the employees. Very seldom did someone pick out a location on just a whim; they might have heard about it from an employee who saw that the safe was left open all day or from a cashier who told them how much money they kept under their drawers.

So we cut that risk off at the source. I made it a personal goal to only hire family-oriented employees: people who would work to the best of their ability and whom we would work hard for in return, paying fair wages and developing a family atmosphere so they wanted to stay. It was this family network model that kept us safe far and above the selective product exclusions and sale prices; good people will always run the bad ones out of town.

JANE »

So many of the people we worked with at Wagner's were close to my heart. They shared the same sense of companionship and support, always looking out for each other and ready to help at a moment's notice, regardless of whether that help was pitching in to cover shifts or lending a friendly ear. We cared for each other like family, and I know our customers sensed that when they came in.

Sherrill was one of those amazing people who had a lasting impact on my life. Whereas Tom, our first butcher, gave me a curiosity about the world, it was Sherrill who sparked my curiosity in religion.

Catholic only because of my family, I gave little thought to the dynamics of the church until Sherrill began to share her faith and insights with me. She was a Seventh Day Adventist, and the passion she had for the Bible and her belief flickered my own flame of desire to learn more about my religion.

For twenty years Sherrill worked with us, starting as a cashier whom I had to teach how to use a calculator and eventually taking over as chief of operations. I will forever be thankful for her. If it hadn't been for her passion, I never would have pursued religious studies. She pushed me to understand my own religion in the same way Tom pushed me to understand things about the world that I'd taken for granted, such as the Interstate signs.

As much as we felt that we were helping our community by giving good jobs, better salaries, fair prices, and respectable places to shop, our community was helping us, too. We could not have been Wagner's Meat without our remarkable employees.

Arm Wrestling with the Long Arm of the Law

SCOTT»

My run-ins with the government began early on and never quite went away. Jane would say it's because I'm the kind of person who "does" and then asks forgiveness later. That may be, but when it comes to business, waiting for months to hear back from government offices about whether or not you have "permission" for a marketing campaign pretty much kills the deal. As an entrepreneur, I'm always trying to offer niche products and services that would take our giant national competitors months or even years to develop. I could never compete on price, but I knew I could move with a speed they could never match. If it worked … let it be written. If it didn't, we stopped.

BEER-BIASED BUREAUCRACY

SCOTT»

Because our Wagner's Meat stores were located at the epicenter of poverty in Louisiana, we were naturally heavily dependent on food stamps—that is, government welfare, or what is known today as EBT (Electronic Benefits Transfer). Now, food stamps are supposed to work the same as cash, and in fact, there are laws in place that say you can't discriminate between a person paying in cash and a person paying with EBT.

Of course, that's what they said. But I seem to have a talent for finding the gray areas when it comes to government.

One year, just as we were about to hit peak summer grilling season, an idea struck me: why not give away a case of beer with any meat special? Sure, we'd figure out a way to work the cost of the beer into the price of the meat, but the customer didn't care. That was the businessman's burden to bear. All they cared about was that they could buy two pounds of burger meat, either with cash or EBT, and it came with the perfect drink pairing for *free*. Try that, chain grocery stores!

A few months later, though, my campaign caught the eye of the local United States Department of Agriculture office, and one day the slow, bureaucratic beast came knocking.

"Oh no, you can't do that!" the USDA rep said. "You can't accept food stamps for meat specials and give away beer. That's the same as accepting food stamps for beer, and if you don't stop, we'll cite you and take away your license."

"So what you're telling me," I argued, "is that someone with cash can buy meat and get free beer, but an EBT customer can't? Isn't that discrimination?"

"You just can't do that," the rep replied. "You can't accept food stamps for meat if you're going to give away beer."

I probably should have stopped. I knew in my gut that if they really wanted to, they could shut me down, but I was young and dumb and on a quest to conquer the food industry. So not only did we continue to accept EBT for meat specials with free beer attached, I started promoting it in our monthly flyers.

Months went by and I didn't hear anything.

I must've really shown them, I thought. I wonder ... what else can I do that the big box stores are afraid to touch?

Then one day the mail carrier asked me to sign a certified letter from the USDA. It took me a while to open that one. Certified letters are never good news, and when I finally sucked it up and tore it open, it was exactly what I'd expected.

"Your establishment has been cited for violation of the USDA food stamp laws, and a hearing has been scheduled ..." blah, blah, blah. In sum, "You better lawyer up!"

For a brief moment there, I thought the other stores who'd jumped on the "free beer" bandwagon would join me in the fight, but no, all I got was "Good luck, Scott. Let us know if we have to stop giving away beer too."

74

Even my lawyer seemed to agree with them.

"Why don't you just agree to stop giving away beer to food stamp customers?" he asked. "If you do, they might drop the charges."

I shook my head. "I'm not backing down on this one. I know I'm right. I'm going to push this envelope just a bit further."

Weeks went by, and I continued to give beer away to food stamp customers, who were clearly on our side judging by the sheer number of sales, but judgment day was fast approaching.

About a week before the hearing, however, we were surprised to receive a notice from the USDA stating that they wanted to postpone. For the life of me, I couldn't figure out why. Even stranger was the fact that they didn't propose a new hearing date.

Months went by and ... crickets. No letters, no visits, no hearing notifications, nothing. I started to wonder if we'd actually won. Had David finally slain Goliath? If so, Goliath wasn't admitting it. But then again, he wasn't challenging us to another round either.

It was years before I found out what really happened. The USDA didn't want a hearing because a hearing would be public. The proceeding would be recorded, and if I'd lost, I could have appealed, bringing the whole thing to the glaring attention of the public eye. What's more, it would have created new case law that they'd have to battle with in the future. It was a flood gate they didn't want to open.

I called it a victory.

Pushing the Envelope

JANE »

Scott wasn't a rule breaker, he was a survivor. He didn't worry about the fangs of government regulations; he just knew what needed to be done in order to survive and did it. It was how he grew up, and I suppose that's the kind of action that never leaves you.

As a kid, Scott's family often had to stretch dollars, paying only the most critical bills when things got too thin. He and his brothers found a survival technique when the city shut their water off. As soon as the water meter truck turned the corner out of sight, the boys would grab the special meter key they had and turn it right back on.

That kind of home life contributed to his tenacity and bravery, and it taught him to take on things bigger than himself. It's one of those qualities that, as a couple, we struggle over. He's always willing to push the envelope and push it hard, but it's the same quality we needed to survive in business.

Those meat specials sold like hotcakes!

As I had the opportunity to acquire a higher education, I began to see things Scott did not see. We were not the smartest business people in the world per se, but we prospered because the government gave people food stamps. Even though Scott constantly declares that government is not a friend of business, inside the classroom at Harvard Divinity School I came to the realization of why we, a couple of teenagers with nothing but GEDs, prospered. We were successful business people because we had grown up in households that talked the language of business, and we sold a lot of meat because the government made sure people in the inner-city neighborhoods were not starving! The United States Department of Agriculture was not happy with our "free" beer

> **The United States Department of Agriculture was not happy with our "free" beer marketing tool, but we thought, Why can't the food stamp customer be treated the same as a cash customer?**

marketing tool, but we thought, Why can't the food stamp customer be treated the same as a cash customer? The government took us to task, and we pushed for everybody getting treated the same.

Besides being a facilitator of food, Wagner's was the neighborhood's bank. This is something I did not grasp until I had time to reflect upon in school. It seemed like everybody in the entire neighborhood was getting a check!

The majority of our customers did not have a checking account because there was not a bank anywhere close. We cashed so many social security and welfare checks. There was so much cash in my trunk going back and forth to the bank, I often wonder how I didn't get picked off. Surely, everyone knew I was shuffling in the cash on check-cashing day.

There were pivotal elements that enabled us to be successful in business. Of course, we did not gamble, drink, or do drugs, but the most important element is the neighborhood looked out for us. I know this in my gut. We had lots of cash, lots of discipline, and most importantly, lots of honest employees.

❖ ❖ ❖

HELLO, DOL

SCOTT»

It was early 1999, and with about three hundred employees between our ten locations, our annual payroll was significant. So when a certified letter from the Department of Labor (DOL) showed up in our mailbox, I wasn't too surprised.

"Your business has been selected at random for an audit," it read.

Sure.

I handed the letter to my accountant Jay and promptly forgot about it. Why should I worry? We used a nationwide payroll company and ran a pretty tight ship.

It wasn't until a few months later that Jay dropped by and told me that the DOL was looking for more records, time punch details from the computer we used for clocking employees in and out.

Okay, I thought. That's unusual, but we'll give them what they want.

Several weeks later, Jay caught up with me again, and this time he looked worried.

"They want to interview all of the employees," he said.

"All of them?" I asked, trying not to look shocked.

Jay nodded. "We better let them, Scott. You don't want to upset the DOL."

Once again we complied, but now I was worried about where this was going.

It took six weeks for the DOL to finish their audits and interviews, and every employee I spoke to reported the same thing: all they did was ask about their daily duties. Harmless, right?

Then Judgment Day arrived.

Jay and I reported to the DOL office on Poydras Street in downtown New Orleans, where two DOL agents escorted us to an empty conference room. A few minutes later, a man with a stony face and quiet personality walked in, pulled up a chair, and jumped right to the point.

"Mr. Wolfe," he said, "the good news is that we did a three-year audit, and the only thing we found was about fifteen thousand dollars owed in back pay to your employees for improper clocking.

"The bad news," he added as he put down his papers and looked me right in the eye, "is that we found twenty-six violations of child labor laws."

I was sure I hadn't heard him correctly.

"Twenty-six violations of what now?" I asked.

"Mr. Wolfe, you have sixteen- and seventeen-year-old children using a motorized slicer to cut meat for customers. It is against the law for anyone under the age of eighteen to operate those machines, which puts you in clear violation of child labor laws," he said. "And each of those violations incurs a ten-thousand-dollar fine."

I jumped out of my seat, ignoring the pleading "Don't get angry" look on Jay's face, and leaned as far as I could toward the stone-faced DOL agent.

"This is a freaking joke, right?" I said.

Out of the corner of my eye, I saw Jay slump back and cover his face.

"Millions of dollars in payroll, and this is what you find? You want to fine me two hundred and sixty thousand dollars for giving jobs to inner-city kids?"

I was so angry I couldn't see straight, but the stone-faced DOL agent didn't flinch.

"Damn it, Jay! Who the hell do these people think they are?"

Jay got up and looked at the agent.

"Maybe you should give us a minute," he said.

The agent nodded and left.

"This is insane!" I said, tossing the stack of government papers across the empty table. "How can I be penalized for hiring teenagers part-time?"

I was pacing the room, fuming.

"Scott, it's okay," Jay replied, doing his best to calm me. "We can appeal this. It's not the end of the world. Let's not get into more trouble."

❖ ❖ ❖

"CAN MY FIVE-YEAR-OLD WORK AT WAGNER'S?"

SCOTT »

Thank God for sleep. It's a great reset button.

I still wasn't thrilled when I woke up the next day, but I was approaching a begrudging acceptance of the DOL's ruling when the phone rang. It was 7:00 a.m.

"Mr. Wolfe?" a female voice asked.

"Yes?"

"This is Sherryl from WVUE News. I'm calling to get your reaction to the child labor law violations."

I had to bite my lip to keep from shouting a thoroughly inappropriate response. What the hell?

"Where did you hear that?" I finally asked.

"The Department of Labor," she said. "They sent out a press release this morning."

I took her number and told her I'd call back. Within half an hour, every single local news station, on air and in print, had called, asking for my response. I knew what I wanted to say—how ridiculous the charges were, how I was giving inner-city kids a chance and a way to stay off the street—but instead I asked Jay what he thought, and he thought we should talk to a labor lawyer.

I should have listened to my gut.

Within hours I was doing what the lawyer told me to do, telling the press, "No comment" and signing off on a noncommittal written statement that might as well have read, "Guilty as charged."

> Within hours I was doing what the lawyer told me to do, telling the press, "No comment" and signing off on a noncommittal written statement that might as well have read, "Guilty as charged."

This was the first time since we had opened Wagner's that I wished we *weren't* the talk of the town. We were the lead story on the evening news and on the front page in the local and state newspapers. The news radio stations couldn't stop talking about us, and even the jock rock stations were kicking us in the shins with jokes like, "Hey, my kid just turned five. Think he could get a job at Wagner's?"

It was a full year before we finally settled the case, with both sides signing an agreement that basically said, "Neither party admits guilt or innocence." Even though we settled for far less than the original fines, it still didn't feel like much of a win. The DOL had targeted us for a witch hunt, and as far as the community was concerned, we'd been burned at the stake.

JANE »

On this day, I watched Scott's heart harden. The law had spoken. Wagner's Meat would no longer so easily hire sixteen- and seventeen-year-old teenagers. After the Department of Labor had snatched their pound of flesh, we were concerned what the neighborhood would think of us. For the very first time in business, I felt concerned.

The next morning, the *Times-Picayune* 🔍 newspaper plastered the government's actions and fines against us, and it would be the mothers of the community that rallied around us. In their eyes, we felt like rock stars. They told us we were doing what we could to provide much-needed jobs to their children. Yes, they agreed teenagers used the deli slicer to cut massive amounts of bologna and luncheon meat, but we helped teenagers stay off the streets.

On this day, we were **burned at the stake** 🔍 by the government, but the mothers of the Ninth Ward neighborhood saved us. It was one of the warmest feelings of neighborhood communion I've ever experienced. Here, I learned, people want you to just do what you can.

❖ ❖ ❖

UNLESS YOU'RE
A CAT 5 HURRICANE

SCOTT »

August 23, 2005.

There was electricity in the air on the days leading up to **Hurricane Katrina.** 🔍 We didn't know what to expect, but as the storm grew larger and more powerful on the radar—and the meteorologist couldn't hide the look of fear in her eyes anymore—a vague sense of panic began to weave its way into the static.

You could feel it the most in the stores. More customers were planning to evacuate than ever before, and the grocery business was booming; we couldn't put water, bread, or canned goods on the shelves fast enough. Funny, I thought, that all these people who were planning to leave were buying emergency survival goods, but I wasn't going to argue with them.

Two days before estimated landfall, the mayor called for a mandatory evacuation.

Jane found me a few hours after the announcement, worry filling her eyes.

"We need to leave," she said.

"You should leave," I told her. "Me and my brothers will say here in case something happens to the properties."

But God bless it, Jane had her way. Mandatory means mandatory, and it means everyone, she insisted. The law won't let you stay.

So we hopped in the car and drove to Alabama to stay with our daughter in her college apartment.

I remember thinking what a waste of time the trip was and how much we'd be out after three or four days of mandatory closure. I had no idea how much our lives were going to change in the next twenty-four hours.

Gone

SCOTT»

If an arsonist had burned down every one of our locations on the same night, we would have been better off. At least it would have spared our neighborhood—at least the market share could have survived.

Ten commercial parcels of real estate, each one as diversified as I could make them, and multiple mortgaged properties, all of them bringing in comfortable lease payments—Katrina took all of it.

New Orleans got a lot of the press for flooding after the storm had passed, but the reality was that only 60 percent of the city went underwater. It was the Ninth Ward, and our hometown, Chalmette, that were hit the worst. One hundred percent submersion.

For days and weeks afterward, we called each other (in a town of seventy-five thousand, it's hard not to know most everyone by name) and asked for news. Everyone had lost their homes, their businesses, their jobs, in a day. In Blue Ridge, Georgia—a small town where a friend allowed use of his vacation home—we called our friends and relatives on the spotty cell service, more often than not getting a frustrating "busy" signal as thousands of calls tried to shove their way through the cell towers.

We didn't find out until almost two weeks later that Jane's grandmother, Ms. Morales, had drowned; she was one of the thirty-five victims at **St. Rita's Nursing Home** 🔍 who had lost their lives when the New Orleans levees broke.

Jane took it hard. Only a few short days after we heard the news, we were in the emergency room at Georgia's Emory Hospital. Jane fought so hard to stay positive, but as the bad news kept rolling in, it was getting the best of her.

JANE »

It took three weeks for Katrina to sink in—what had happened, what we'd lost, what everyone lost. I'd talked with my mother before the storm hit about moving Grandma. But Mom insisted that she was safe.

"They're equipped to handle storms," Mom said, referring to St. Rita's. "Can you imagine how difficult an evacuation will be on a ninety-year-old? If they really feel that they need to move everyone, they will, but they don't want to put them through that trauma."

When I found out how she had died, how all thirty-five of those residents had died in a sudden flood, I had to blame someone ... so I blamed her.

The first conversation I had with her after the storm was brutal. I can't remember exactly what I said, but there came a point in the call where Dad took the phone out of her hands and said to me, very calmly, "This is your mother you're talking to, Jane. And she just lost her mother. You shouldn't be talking to her like this."

It wasn't until later that I learned how St. Rita's had assured Mom that they *were* moving the residents and then didn't.

Without realizing it, I slipped into an emotional fog. I wasn't worried about our finances. And I wasn't concerned about our physical losses. My thought was simply that we would "go in and clean up," no big deal.

But the emotions drained me. Scott's mother was struggling with the memories of Hurricane Betsy, which had hit just south of New Orleans in 1965. She couldn't believe that she had to live through that kind of devastation again. I gave her a listening ear and uplifting words, but I wouldn't know what she meant until weeks later, when they finally let us return home.

My sister, too, couldn't hold back the tears. Days after the storm passed, I was sitting in a parking lot, trying to console her over the phone.

"We've lost everything," she said. "We don't know what we're going to do."

The skating rink she had run for more than a decade in the small town of Chalmette was gone, and I was doing everything I could to lift her up, including reminding her that her husband had gotten his contractor license at just the right time.

"It will all be fine, Jean," I remember telling her. "Everyone is going to need him out there. You don't even have to worry about that rink."

There was my momma, too, who needed my shoulder as much as I needed hers, and the quiet support I gave to Scott and his brothers. I shouldered so much emotion that I slowly began to lose my own. And as the fog settled, I found that I couldn't stop shaking inside myself. It was only a little bit at first, but it wouldn't stop. I couldn't sleep and couldn't stop the feeling of shaking even if I could stop it physically.

I don't remember Scott taking me to the emergency room in

Georgia, only a few miles from the cabin we were staying in. They ran an IV and asked dozens of questions.

A few hours passed. It was quiet, and I was just closing my eyes to rest when I heard soft voices through the privacy curtain next to me. It was an elderly couple, New Orleans refugees like ourselves, and the woman was doing her best to explain her husband's condition to the doctor. He was in the midst of cancer treatment, she was telling him, and he couldn't miss a session. But they couldn't go home for his next treatment, as there was nothing for them to go home to. They'd lost everything.

Just like that, the shakes were gone. When the nurse came in a little while later, I told her I was ready to leave.

"You don't need to treat me anymore. Go treat them," I said, pointing to the curtained room beside me. "They need more help than I do."

They sent me home that day with a bottle of sleeping pills and a diagnosis of anxiety. I took two of them over the next two days just to help me sleep, but after that I was fine. The anxiety was gone—it had finally sunk in what had happened. Everything was gone. Our grocery stores were lost, our employees were homeless and jobless, and the neighborhoods where we had properties ... was gone. I never knew what it meant to suffer from anxiety until that moment, but now I understand. It was one of several hard lessons that Katrina taught us that year.

An Empty Road to the Unfamiliar

SCOTT »

As a business owner, I was given a pass to return to New Orleans ahead of the general population. I kissed Jane goodbye and left her in Georgia at the cabin. I wanted to make sure everything was safe, that our house was at least somewhat livable, before I brought her home.

The main interstate through Louisiana to New Orleans was still closed, so I took an old state highway that followed the bayous instead. My headlights seemed dim in the pitch dark, and a distinct smell leaked through the air conditioner.

As I neared Chef's Pass, I could see emergency lights flickering in the distance. The bright white of military vehicle headlights flooded the road, and as I approached, a uniformed young man with an automatic rifle slung across his arm gestured for me to stop.

"This road is closed," he said as I rolled down the window. Behind him, a row of four or five troops eyed my car and kept their hands cautiously on their gun stocks. I suddenly felt like I'd been transported to another country, another time. Was I driving toward my home or German-occupied France? I held up the official documents verifying that I was a business owner and that I was allowed to pass. The young man looked them over carefully, then gestured to the troops behind him, who immediately stepped out of the way.

"Be safe," he said.

Silent. Dark. Lonely. The road unwound in front of me like a scene from a horror film. Massive trees, skeletal in the pale wash of my headlights, loomed on the sides of the road, fresh gashes streaking their sides from where the bulldozers had pushed them out of the way. The air was intense, swampy, and for the first time I noticed that there were no sounds—no birds, no traffic, no horns, not even insects. It was like driving slowly through the Grand Canyon. I heard nothing.

As I neared home, I stopped at the on-ramp to I-10 at Chef Menteur Highway and parked in the middle of the empty road, not just because I could but because something had caught my eye on the blue flyover exit sign. I had to make sure I wasn't seeing things.

The sign, raised high enough for the biggest eighteen-wheelers to pass under, was some twenty-two feet off the ground, and there, just above the reflective words "New Orleans," was a grimy dark floodwater line with a bit of seaweed stuck just above the "s."

It was a surreal moment.

I'd heard about the flooding and seen videos and pictures of it, but I wasn't prepared to see a waterline so far above the ground in person. For the first time, I was truly scared about what I would find when I drove home.

Like a Giant Melted S'mores Bar

SCOTT»

I pulled up at our headquarters at the corner of Elysian Fields and I-610 and left the car running in the parking lot, headlights pointed at the storefront.

The light seemed unusually bright as I rummaged around for my keys, until I noticed that it was reflecting off of a thick smear of mineral deposit on the plate glass window. A few seconds after I found the keys, I also found out that they were useless—the lock was frozen, rusted shut.

I used the edge of my shirtsleeve to wipe away some of the gray grit on the window and shone a small flashlight into the room…and for a moment, **I couldn't process what I was seeing.** ⊗

The same thick, gray mineral sludge that had crusted over the window was also covering every last inch of the store. It looked like a giant s'mores bar had melted over everything or like the inside of a ship that had sank centuries ago. I took a few steps back and looked around at my neighboring businesses; Burger King, Cox Cable Company, all deserted, all covered in the same gray mud.

Getting back in the car, I drove slowly around the neighborhood, assessing the damage. Whole houses were gone, and others looked like the next breeze would knock them over. Cars were overturned in the streets, and everywhere the same gray sludge covered everything. It was as though the mud had frozen the city in time. After a while I stopped the car and just sat there, headlights pointed at the empty, muddy, soundless streets. I was not prepared for what I saw, and my mind was vacant on where to start.

> **Whole houses were gone, and others looked like the next breeze would knock them over.**

❖ ❖ ❖

INSURANCE, FEMA, AND THE CABBAGE STRATEGY

SCOTT»

We could take out $2.5 million in Small Business Administration (SBA) loans.

That was the word circulating among business owners. Thirty-year loans at a 2 percent rate. If that was true, I thought, we'd actually *make* money on this storm! But as with all government programs, our stores were square pegs trying to fit in round holes. We spent six months filing applications only to wind up shelling out $375,000 to cover mortgage payments on our abandoned properties and then spending another $200,000 just to gut and board up our ten locations, without a dollar to be seen from the Federal Emergency Management Agency (FEMA).

And with no word on whether FEMA would help with rebuilding the local roads and utilities, we were stuck between a rock and a hard place. There was no point reinvesting in our properties if no one could get to them. Yet meanwhile we were losing money hand over fist as we paid six-figure monthly mortgages with no income to replace it.

Our only hope was in insurance—and of course, those documents, and the computer they were also stored on, were covered in the same gray muck that covered everything.

It took time, but gradually my insurance agent (who was obviously very busy) sent copies of my policies. All but one location had flood insurance, so we put the insurance company on notice and waited for the stream of adjusters to arrive.

As they showed up, one by one, each of them walked in with the same questions: What was caused by flood and what was caused by wind? Since the flood insurance was underwritten by the federal government, the private wind insurers were doing everything they could to blame damages on the flood.

Then there were the inventory and equipment claims. The adjusters held out their hands asking for receipts, and all I could do was point at the pile of mud that was once a line of filing cabinets. You want receipts? I said. You're gonna have to start digging.

It was the beginning of a long, exhausting fight for insurance money that ended in a lose-lose option: we could either take their offer of 50 percent of the value of everything we'd lost or we could hire on attorney to fight it and end up paying the attorney the extra 50 percent we won.

The insurance companies had mastered the cabbage strategy long ago: let 'em cook. Eventually the consumer would run out of cash, get desperate, and accept the ridiculously low offer.

Thank God Scott Jr. decided to go into law. For three years he fought to get us full payment from the wind insurance companies. Meanwhile, the banks quickly lost their sympathy and instituted a zero-tolerance policy on late mortgage payments. In fact, we were hit with an unexpected curveball when we discovered that the insurance proceeds that Scott Jr. had won for us required two signatures: mine and the bank's. This often triggered a tug-of-war, as the bank wanted the insurance proceeds to pay down our debt, whereas I wanted it to pay for repairs and to fund our new company, **Wolfman Construction.** Q

❖ ❖ ❖

TURNING ON WOLFMAN CONSTRUCTION

SCOTT »

I grew up in a construction family.

My father was a contractor for his entire career, from working as the director of construction for Popeye's Chicken in the late 1970s to building dozens of custom homes and commercial buildings around New Orleans with me and my brothers. T.E. Wolfe and Sons, Inc, he called it, and from an early age, every one of us worked in some form or other for the family business.

Being the youngest of the five, I often just helped by cleaning up, painting, and picking up materials for the tradesmen, a quarter-inch shoe molding here or a two-by-four there. I didn't realize until we started doing new construction for Wagner's that I'd retained a lot of that construction knowledge. So much so, in fact, that I decided to apply for my own contractor license and open Wolfman Construction. It was convenient when we were building so many new stores … and it was our saving grace in the wake of the storm.

It was some six months after Katrina before we were able to gut and renovate our company headquarters, that first s'mores-covered wreck I had visited when I came back to New Orleans. Getting the power on alone was a miracle, one that cost me a hundred bucks more than I had expected.

For weeks the word was that Entergy Electric, the local electricity company, was restoring service to our street, but none of us could get a representative on the phone to schedule an electrician. Then one day I spotted an Entergy truck driving down the street and immediately flagged it over.

The electrician raised a cautious eyebrow as I trotted up.

"Hey man," I said, slightly out of breath from running after his van. "Look, all we need is someone to flip the main breakers up there." I pointed to the top of the electric pole next to our building.

The electrician glanced at the pole and immediately shook his head.

"No way," he said. "That's three-phase energy you need turned on. I have to break out the dead poles, gloves, the whole deal. I don't have the time."

I sighed and pulled out my wallet.

"Will a hundred change your mind?"

We had the power on in fifteen minutes.

As the building filled with light for the first time in more than half a year, I felt like a kid on Christmas. We were finally ready for business.

❖ ❖ ❖

A ROOF OVER NEW ORLEANS

SCOTT »

We had our headquarters back, but it was no longer headquarters for Wagner's Meat. We were now home base for Wolfman Construction, and we were booking **roofing jobs** faster than we could answer the phone.

I don't know what we would have done if we hadn't established Wolfman Construction before the storm had hit. As it was, we didn't exactly decide to go into the roofing business. But as we waited for insurance claims to process, roads to be repaired, and residents to come back home, we went where the work was…and reason dictated that anyone looking to move back into a home or business would make sure the building was watertight before doing any kind of renovation.

The thing was that while we had our administration completely staffed up—salesperson, estimator, bookkeeper, and supplier—what we didn't have were roofers. And with just about every building in New Orleans suffering roof damage, finding roofers to work for us was about as easy as finding a polar bear in a snowstorm.

JANE »

We didn't know we were going into the roofing business until we were in it. Scott had a contractor's license for years, of course, but it had never occurred to me that it might replace Wagner's. To me, Wolfman was just Scott's side business, his way of staying on top of the building costs of new grocery locations.

But then one day, a few months after the storm had passed and not long after residents had been allowed to come back to the area, we found ourselves driving up and down the streets of uptown New Orleans with Scott's mother and father in the back seat. We were just taking it all in—the damage, the wreckage of buildings, the gray muck still covering everything—when suddenly Scott pulled the car over and jumped out.

He'd seen a couple standing outside their home, staring up at their damaged roof with worried looks. Scott walked right up to them and shook their hands, and I heard him say, "Looks like your roof needs to be fixed."

I walked up just in time to hear the next unbelievable words out of his mouth.

"You know, we have a roofing company," he said and smiled. "We can take care of that for you!"

Roofing company? I thought, surprised. Since when did we have a roofing company?

Then I saw him take one of his old Wolfman Construction cards out of his wallet, and just like that, I saw his vision for recovering from the loss of our ten stores. The dozens of people we drove by all staring at their roofs with the same concerned look, the couple, the construction business … it made perfect sense.

Just like that, we were selling. We'd drive up to a cluster of home-owners, hop out, and start telling them about our roofing company.

There was no discussion about making roofing our next step, no long couple's planning talk about the pros and cons, who would handle what, etc. We shared nothing more than an understanding look, and by the time we finished that drive, with Scott's very surprised parents in tow, we had twenty jobs lined up.

All we needed now was a roofing crew.

* * *

Getting into the roofing business was fun because it was raw. We'd been in business for twenty-five years before Katrina hit and were at least two decades beyond the need to knock on doors and cold-call people. Then suddenly we were walking up and down sidewalks, peddling our services, and I couldn't stop smiling. I didn't know I still had cold calls in me; I didn't know *we* still had it in us.

Finding crews to build the roofs, too, turned out to be less of a challenge than we had expected. Perhaps it was because we understood, after a quarter century in business, how important it is to treat fellow human beings with respect.

I started walking to the corners and parking lots where roofing crews would wait to be picked up and driven to the job site for the day, and I'd just say to them, "Hey! Do you want a better paying job and a company that treats you with respect? We're hiring." And I'd hand out our card.

Inevitably one or two of the guys would ask me what we were paying, and my answer was always "Whatever you're being paid now, we'll do better."

It didn't take long before we had a full-time crew of more than thirty workers repairing roofs all over the greater New Orleans area, and the same family atmosphere from Wagner's pulled together a new family at Wolfman Construction. We were repairing homes and offices, government facilities, even historic buildings, and we became one of the top private construction companies in New Orleans.

Speaking of historic buildings, there was one roof repair that almost ended our second chance at success in a single night.

Torching Down the Palace

SCOTT»

It was 6:00 a.m. and the sun was just starting to rise above the French Quarter skyline when a wisp of smoke like a papal decree caught my eye ... and I instantly got a sinking feeling in my stomach.

It was the day after we finished replacing a torch-down roof for restaurateur Dickie Brennan's Palace Cafe, a classy modern creole restaurant at the foot of Bourbon Street housed within the beloved former Werlein's Music store where Louis Armstrong used to get his trumpets.

It was a difficult job. A torch-down roof is the most dangerous roof to replace, as it requires the roofers to torch down a thick layer of tar. Because of the live fire, roofers tend to finish around 4:00 p.m. and then wait two hours with a fire extinguisher on the roof, just to make sure there aren't any hot embers under the roof line.

That's what we did too. The crew finished at four, and per protocol, stuck around until six to confirm that the roof wasn't going to catch on fire.

But it did.

Two minutes after I saw the dark thread of smoke drift up from the French Quarter, my phone starting ringing.

It was Richie, our new chief operating officer. "The Palace Cafe is on fire," he said. "I'm picking you up. Be there in five."

There were Mardi Gras–level crowds by the time we got there. All the people in the surrounding buildings were rubbernecking on their balconies or on the street, trying to get a closer look at the fire. Six fire trucks were parked in front of the main structure, and most of them had their ladders up. Firefighters were walking on the roof in full gear with pickaxes, while at least three local TV stations filmed the action from a street median.

From inside Richie's SUV, we watched as the fire roared out of the third-floor windows, rolling onto the roof where the firefighters stood. All I could think was, *My God, please don't let one of them fall through.*

That building had to be worth at least $10 million. Our company, on the other hand, only had $2 million in general liability insurance. Even as the firefighters doused the flames and the smoke cleared, I was convinced that we were out of business that day.

Fortunately, the damage wasn't as bad as the flames, crowds, and media coverage had let on. The water and firefighters actually caused more harm to the building than the fire, with the worst of it centralized in Dickie Brennan's personal office. The restaurant on the first floor never closed, and we were able to repair the roof within a week … and we still made a profit! It was a miracle; and it was the same day Wolfman Construction passed a policy to never repair torch-down roofs again.

IN HOT WATER WITH THE NAVY

S C O T T »

"Scott, we have a problem."

That's not the first thing anyone wants to hear, especially not the owner of a contracting company, and especially not from the head of the largest disaster recovery service in North America, and especially not in relation to repair work done on the roof protecting the US Navy's worldwide computer payroll system.

I took a deep breath and tried to sound casual.

"And what would that be?" I asked.

"The parapet walls," he said. "It seems you guys damaged them, and we're going to need to withhold part of your payment until it's replaced."

"I see," I said, starting to pace the room. "And how much is that going to be?"

"A hundred and twenty thousand dollars."

The guy barely had a chance to set the phone down before I was standing at the front doors of the building in question, the University of New Orleans Technology Center, with my leadership team. I had to see this damage for myself.

Sure enough, he was right. There were dents and scrapes on all the panels. But how? I'd been mother-henning this job since I had found out about the navy's $100 million computer system within (on the top floor, of all places). So when did it happen?

Then it hit me. Before we found out about the high-risk hardware, I'd taken close to three hundred photos of the project in preparation of bidding, including pictures of the parapet walls. On reviewing the images (each of which were date stamped, thank goodness), we found that the parapet walls were damaged before we ever started work. That one little pre-smartphone detail saved our company $120,000.

Finally, a Customer Who Doesn't Complain ... Me!

SCOTT»

Then, six years after Katrina hit, I woke up one morning and decided I was done.

It was too much. Since 2006 we'd completed hundreds of construction jobs and done more than $30 million in work, and on that particular morning I opened my eyes to thirty jobs going on simultaneously, thirty employees with families to feed, and a liability exposure that made me flinch every time the phone rang, worrying that this would be the call that ended everything.

I was tired of it. All I wanted was to go back to one employee and one customer: me.

We didn't shut the doors that day. Instead, Jane and I agreed to simply stop taking orders and to slowly reduce the workforce until it was just us. Our construction company had done what we needed it to do—it had rescued our real estate nest egg, paid for our lifestyle, and even helped put the lives of my brother Mike and cousin Richie back together. It was a blessing to have that contractor license when we did, and by 2012, we'd recovered in full.

We also decided that we weren't going back to our former, twenty-four-hour seven-days-a-week grocery business either. We'd had enough of effectively running a small country around the clock. We wanted to finish work at 5:00 p.m. And have Sundays off. That wasn't a lot to ask, was it?

So I started doing something I had always wanted to do: developing real estate. I bought and renovated a property on Broad Street, turning it into an auto parts store, turned a property on St. Claude Avenue into a convenience store and deli, turned a property on Elysian Fields into a chain retail store, and purchased and transformed several other properties.

Then one day, a closed dry cleaner caught my eye.

It was right across the street from a popular Family Dollar store. There was plenty of heavy traffic, easy parking, and lots of rooftops. All it needed was a concept.

That old excitement from the days of scouting new Wagner's Meat locations started to come back. I could feel the potential of this little shop.

Still, I didn't leap right away. All the years of scouting real estate in this town had taught me a thing or two, and I wasn't in any particular rush. For one, the shop was on the "wrong" side of the street; people coming from New Orleans proper would have to turn left on a highway to pull in. Then there were the development costs, monthly mortgage, gross margins on projected sales—if I was even half wrong in my estimates, would I be able to pay the bills?

I reeled in my initial excitement and decided to tuck the location into a mental back pocket, driving by every few months or so just to look for any signs of advantages or pitfalls. If, after half a year or so, I still felt that same excitement that I had on day one, I told myself that I'd pursue it.

As it turned out, I wasn't the only one considering investing in a dream at the time.

Post-Wolfman Construction, my passion for property development was in full swing. Jane, on the other hand, was full swing into empty nest syndrome. Both our children were grown and married, and with no grandchildren as of yet, she had all the time in the world to dwell on it.

Fortunately, Jane also knew how to grab opportunity when she saw it. From the moment I met her, Jane always had a deep love, almost a hunger, for learning. So with time to spare, she decided to do what she loved best in the world. Only a few months after we closed the doors on Wolfman, Jane signed up for continuing education studies at **Tulane University.**

That first day at Tulane is still one of my favorite memories. Jane was like a kindergartener on her first day of school. I watched her walk up those intimidating concrete steps and disappear in the imposing Gothic building at the forefront of Tulane's main campus, proud as I could be. Then suddenly I remembered seeing her as just a kid, when I was just a kid, passing by each other in elementary school. The unexpected memory was so real, it almost brought tears to my eyes.

They say the longest journey starts with the first step, and I was so glad to watch her take it.

Putting Your Heart into It

SCOTT »

I like to joke that Jane got into Tulane through the back door and walked out the front door four years later, but it's true. She's one of the very few people who ever did.

It began with her application to Tulane's continuing education classes. At first, I thought it was just a way for her to fill the void of not running a business and raising children, a healthy use of time but not anything long-term. But as time went on, it became more and more a part of her life. She signed up for more classes, started attending school functions, and made connections with all levels of the school's administration. She introduced me to a world of academia I had never known existed, introducing me to people with academic titles I could barely pronounce, let alone understand. She would talk with them about these high-level concepts, and I just stood there and stared at them like "dick on a fish." It wasn't my world, but it turned out to be practically custom tailored for Jane.

Her first year, Jane got virtually all As, shocking for a girl with nothing more than a GED under her belt. And that track record never changed. Each semester Jane put her all into each class, reading and writing constantly to the point where I was exhausted *for* her, and the As kept pouring in.

Then one day she was a senior. And not just a senior, either, but a senior at Newcomb Tulane, one of the most prestigious schools in the country. The kids were shocked, her parents were proud, and I was downright surprised. Jane had walked into Tulane an empty nester and walked out a **grandmother alumni.** ▣

❖ ❖ ❖

LET HARVARD TELL HER "NO"

S C O T T »

Hooked on knowledge but worn out from years of studying and hitting deadlines, Jane wondered if a master's degree was the right step for her or if she should simply be content with her bachelor's degree. She seemed to be leaning toward the latter until a professor at Tulane planted the idea in her head that she should apply to **Harvard Divinity School.**

She came home that day with a look I recognized, which worried me. It meant that she'd made a big decision, and no matter what I said there was nothing on God's green earth that was going to change her mind.

"I'm applying to Harvard," she said. "It's the school where I'm willing to further my education, and if I don't get in, I'm done."

There was only one answer I could give.

"Okay."

Now, Jane is not your normal college applicant. With more than thirty years of business ownership under her belt, she'd built up a level of entrepreneurial instincts that kids vying for a Harvard business degree would give their left arm to have. At the same time, she'd also learned how to leave a powerful impression. People don't remember businesses that drift quietly by in the night; they remember the ones that stand out, that do something wildly different and make you wonder what you're missing by not being a part of that business in some way, every day.

That was Jane. From the moment she decided to apply at Harvard, she made sure everyone who had a hand in the application process knew who she was and what she was about. We all knew the odds she was facing: only 6 percent of Harvard applicants are accepted each year, and while she graduated *summa cum laude* from a great school, so did most of the candidates she was up against. So she decided to do what she does best: leave a positive impression.

I still don't know how she did it, but Jane was able to get glowing recommendations from both the provost of Tulane and one of her history professors, the famous political operative James Carville. If that wasn't enough, she also sent her application to Harvard in an oversized envelope with a bright yellow smiley face on it along with her professional CV and years of media acknowledgments from our time running Wagner's Meat and Wolfman Construction.

During applicant orientation week, Jane flew to Cambridge and personally introduced herself to the people in charge of admissions. Then, when she returned to New Orleans, she put together gift baskets filled with local spices and treats and mailed them to each of the people she'd met along with a handwritten thank-you card.

Like I said, everyone remembers Jane.

Months passed, and it became eerie waiting for a decision from Harvard. At one point the kids asked me what I was going to do if Mom actually got accepted.

"Are you going to move to Massachusetts?" they asked.

"Don't worry about that," I reassured them. "They have such a low acceptance rate. Let Harvard tell Mama no. Then I won't have to."

❖ ❖ ❖

OF THE NEW THINGS

JANE »

The first time I ever received a **twenty-page syllabus, 🔍** it was from Richard Parker, my professor for religion, politics, and public policy at Harvard University. It would be the first time the word "religion" was used in a class title at the Kennedy School of Government.

I was at a point in my life where my Catholic faith wasn't sitting well with me. I felt like it only gave me part of the story, that there were these giant blanks that, despite all my years in the church, had never been filled in. But then, as I read through this giant syllabus, I saw a note he'd made under the study of Catholicism that read, simply, "Rerum Novarum changed everything."

I considered myself a pretty strong Catholic, and yet I'd never heard about **Rerum Novarum. 🔍** Not a thing.

It was an encyclical, a letter sent to all the ancient Roman Catholic churches, written by Pope Leo XIII in 1891 only a few years after the Civil War and at the dawn of the Industrial Revolution. It was the first time I'd ever seen religion, politics, and economics come together … and it was beautiful.

Rerum Novarum, or "Of the New Things," spoke to the terrible divide between classes, of "the misery and wretchedness pressing so unjustly on the majority of the working class," and about how "working men have been surrendered, isolated and helpless, to the hardheartedness of employers and the greed of unchecked competition." It urged the wealthy to honor their workers, to treat them as human beings, and to allow them to not only earn just enough to survive from day to day but to be able to set something aside so that they, too, may one day be able to pursue a dream.

> We were phenomenally blessed, and yet I wondered... had we truly been proper stewards of God's providence?

But there was one line in particular that absolutely resonated in the core of my being, and it still does to this day.

"Whoever has received from the divine bounty a large share of temporal blessings," it read, "has received them for the purpose of using them for the perfecting of his own nature, and, at the same time, that he may employ them, as the steward of God's providence, for the benefit of others."

That was me. That was *us*.

Over the years, Scott and I had received a remarkable share of "temporal blessings," not once but many times, from Wagner's Meat to Wolfman Construction. We were phenomenally blessed, and yet I wondered … had we truly been proper stewards of God's providence? Had we given what was given to us to benefit others?

Not long after reading this remarkable paper, I dove into the teachings of Monsignor **John A. Ryan.** 🔍 In 1906, Monsignor Ryan wrote his doctoral dissertation, "A Living Wage: Its Ethical and Economic Aspects," which effectively argued for the establishment of a minimum wage so that workers could rely on a base standard of living. The argument, said Father Ryan, wasn't an economic issue as much as it was an ethical one. "The question," he wrote, "is not what a man must have in order to be a profitable producer, but what he ought to have as a human being."

That, along with the Rerum Novarum still tickling my conscious, was what finally made me sit down and ask, "Did we *really* do right by our employees?"

We always paid more than minimum wage at Wagner's and Wolfman, but that wasn't as much of a socially conscious choice as it was a smart business decision. Our employees were much more inclined to work for us at eleven dollars an hour as opposed to the grocery store up the street for nine.

But I didn't believe that was truly the "living wage," as Father Ryan described it.[3] It may have been enough to allow our employees to pay for their basic needs, but was it enough for them to afford a little more than that as well? Was it enough for them to believe in our company beyond the next paycheck? Did they believe that they were more than just another set of hands at our company?

We put encouraging messages to the community up on the readerboards, we gave well paying jobs to many in the community who worked with us for years, we participated and sponsored community events, we gave away free ice cream cones for good report cards, we developed bright and positive places to shop in deserted urban areas, and on and on. We did a lot, and we did good.

---

3   Father Ryan, in pushing for economic planning that would allow workers to earn fair wages, and in turn, spend those wages to the greater benefit of the American economy as a whole, was the driving force behind the establishment of a minimum wage in the United States. In fact, his Bishop's Program of Social Reconstruction, commissioned by the National Catholic War Council in 1919, became President Franklin Roosevelt's inspiration when penning the New Deal and greatly influenced the Fair Labor Standards Act of 1938. SOURCE: https://www.stthomas.edu/cathstudies/cst/about/johnaryan/

But.

As much as I wanted to say "yes," that our employees always felt valued, that Scott and I went out of our way to make sure our team benefited from the company's growth as much as we did…I couldn't. I couldn't say our focus always went beyond the standard bottom line of profit and loss to that all-important *second* bottom line.

We brought love into our business' family and neighborhoods, but did we *start* with love? Did we make the impact we could have? That we should have?

Manners Matter in the Moment

JANE »

Maybe it was because we only had our GEDs when we started Wagner's, or maybe it was just the way we were brought up, but Scott and I never felt or acted as though we were "better than thou" with our employees and customers.

We couldn't help the fact that being business owners meant that others automatically categorized us, mentally placing us in a certain social class, but we never talked down to anyone because we didn't consider ourselves *above* anyone. We engaged with people, not on *their* level, but on *our* level. We were all in this together, making the magic of our stores happen.

I always felt that the way in which Scott treated our employees and customers was a perfect snapshot of our sincerity. He didn't have some secret recipe for building good relationships or bringing up great employees, it was simply the fact that he was always very careful about his manners. From his years working with both our fathers, he knew that there was no such thing as a teachable moment; the lessons were ongoing, and every action set an example for future behavior.

I've never once heard Scott spill a curse word in front of others at work. If an employee needed to be corrected, he did it in such a way that it felt like teaching rather than reprimanding, and when a customer came to him with an honest complaint, he made it right.

I remember Keith, lovingly nicknamed **"Bucket,"** 🔍 one of our meat market workers, once pulling Scott aside and saying, "A customer wants a refund on her chicken."

"Then give it to her," Scott said without a second thought.

"Yeah, but," Bucket said, frustrated, "she wants a refund because she left her chicken in her trunk all night!"

Scott still gave her a refund. In fact, whenever someone returned meat at Wagner's, even if it was already cooked, we offered a refund. This was just one of those decisions we made early on, because in the end, it was far better to lose a couple of dollars and keep a customer happy as opposed to arguing over those same dollars and losing a good customer … and likely our good reputation, as well.

It just came down to good manners.

The manner in which you treat your fellow worker or your fellow customer, the manner in which you tally the cash drawer at the end of the night, and the manner in which you react to the drawer being short, the manner in which you excuse bad decisions such as stealing or sleeping on the job, and the manner in which the business owner reacts in the moment are the lessons that resonate with employees today, tomorrow, and for a lifetime.

Being in the grocery business in the inner city of New Orleans was a nice place to be because everyone was treated equally at the register. It was our opportunity to positively influence our community every day, even though we weren't aware we were doing it. We just knew that treating others with respect and remembering our manners was *the right thing to do.*

Years after we closed the doors on Wagner's from the destruction of Hurricane Katrina, it shouldn't have surprised me to find that we would have yet another chance to meet that second bottom line and to be good stewards of a temporal blessing. Even before I graduated from Harvard Divinity School, Scott had immersed himself in bringing his latest business venture to life. It was a dream he had admittedly refused to see for years, but with the eerie peace and quiet he found himself in after retiring Wolfman Construction, he was finally ready to make another deal. Little did we know that it would soon become the most socially impactful business we'd ever brought to life.

❖ ❖ ❖

EAT AT MELBA'S

SCOTT »

As a business owner for thirty-plus years, I gained a sixth sense about the retail potential of certain properties. Watching the traffic flow, the ease of parking, safety, size, costs, zoning, nearby population—all those little factors helped me see potential where others might just see a broken-down old store front.

Melba's ◙ had been in plain sight for years; I just wasn't ready to see it yet.

It was a few years after we closed Wolfman Construction and quite frankly, I was bored. Jane was off at Harvard getting her master's degree, the kids had their own families keeping them busy, and I had nothing better to do than check in on the properties we owned around town. I wasn't building anything, and that bothered me.

It was only then, when the itch to strike another deal was too much to bear, that I finally saw the odd-shaped little property across from the Family Dollar we owned for what it was: opportunity.

❖ ❖ ❖

FORGET COFFEE, WHAT PEOPLE WANT IS COMFORT

SCOTT »

My first thought was to simply launch a solid business concept in the space and turn it around for a profit. I had a hard time picturing what kind of business would fit in that large, awkwardly shaped space, but then the idea of splitting the building into two suites struck me: one side would be a laundromat and the other a coffee and yogurt shop. I'd try to lease the renovated shell, but if that didn't work, we could open it up, run it for a while, and then lease it.

We fixed it up and waited for the buyers to come knocking our door down, but they never came. The "For Lease" sign stood out front for several months before I finally gave in.

"Looks like we need to open something," I told Jane, so we did.

❖ ❖ ❖

THIS STORE WILL NOT EXIST WITHOUT HEART

JANE »

When Scott first told me he was going to open something in that long-vacant storefront, I knew this was our chance to finally do for our employees what we should have done a long time ago. *I was firm with him.*

"I support opening another retail business." I said, "I know you will work all day and all night on it and you will have upward of forty employees, but if you're not going to pay a **living wage,** I don't want any part of it!"

That was the strength that my time at Harvard Divinity School and Harvard Kennedy School of Government had given me. It cemented the convictions I felt in my heart because I had always been under the impression that minimum wage was not enough.

> Our bottom line had to be based on more than profit; it had to be based on how we were positively affecting society, the community, and the employees.

And even though we had always paid a tick above the minimum wage, what I meant was that we needed to take it even further. Our bottom line had to be based on more than profit; it had to be based on how we were positively affecting society, the community, and the employees. We had to do more than just "open a store." We had to make such a strong, positive impact that it resounded throughout the neighborhood, and especially, with the people.

SCOTT»

The idea was to open both suites and let the coffee shop employees service the laundromat. That meant that if we could get the coffee shop to at least pay for itself, the income from the laundromat would be pure profit.

We knew this because we'd owned three laundromats over the past three decades or so, and every one of them had been adjacent to a convenience store and followed the same structure: convenience store employees serviced the laundromat, and once we'd paid for equipment and labor, the rest was pure profit.

Getting to the "pure profit" point, however, was going to be a hurdle. Laundromats are not cheap to open. To be successful you have to have a lot of machines (people will stop coming if the machines are never available), which costs at least $400,000. Throw in $8,000 per month in labor, and those quarters better be flying into the machines around the clock or you'll never break even.

The other hurdle was the decision to make the storefront a coffee and yogurt café. Even though the demographic reports were against it, it made sense to me at the time; there was no viable coffee or yogurt competition within a three-mile radius, which meant that all coffee and yogurt lovers in that area would be 100 percent ours. All we needed to do was pay for two employees per shift, and the laundromat was the gravy.

It turned out that the demographic reports were right.

Not only was it a terrible location for coffee and yogurt, we couldn't even cover payroll. Shortly after we opened, I estimated that we were losing about $10,000 a month. I still believed in the location, but the concept needed a serious overhaul.

* * *

Whenever I'm at my wits' end, I usually tell Jane the problem. She was finishing up her second-to-last year at Harvard at the time, and it was with fresh eyes and her remarkable intuition that she gave me the perfect solution.

"Go back to the Wagner's model," she said. "Add **po-boys** and all that home-cooked food we used to sell in the delis inside the grocery, and I'll bet you we can turn that location around."

Of course. It made all the sense in the world. That was what our friends and neighbors were looking for, and we had twenty-something years of experience perfecting those recipes.

But that decision meant we faced yet another serious hurdle: we had to retool, renovate, and restock the entire store from the ground up. We needed new equipment, hoods, fryers, stoves, and coolers, and we also had to reintroduce our store to the public.

Thankfully, a lot of factors fell into place to make the turnaround possible. Jane was nearing her final year at Harvard, which meant that all my energy could be focused on the rebuild instead of splitting time between New Orleans and Cambridge. At the same time, my brother Keith was ending his career at Walgreens and was looking for a new opportunity. I wasn't keen on bringing family into the business, as I still wasn't sure if the store would survive the overhaul, but Jane talked me into it.

"He needs you and you need him," she assured me.

So we met and laid down some ground rules.

Keith would take the helm, we agreed, and deal with the customers and employees so I could concentrate on big-picture issues such as menu development, renovations, and marketing.

I also wanted to make sure Keith had the strongest team possible working with him, so I began reaching out to our former Wagner's employees, and **Lois** 🔍 (pronounced "Loy-s") was at the top of my list.

Lois worked with us for more than fifteen years and was an amazing cook. She knew and trusted us, and we trusted her to the ends of the earth. Trouble was, though, that we'd lost touch with most of the former Wagner's employees, including Lois, after Katrina blew through.

It took some time, but we finally found her in Houston, Texas, cooking for a retirement home. She'd gotten married after the storm and was hesitant to move.

"That's okay," I told her on the phone. "Bring him here too. I'll find you a place."

But still, she was reluctant. It wasn't until months later, when she dropped by the store during a visit to her relatives, that she finally agreed to move back to New Orleans and work for us again. Ever since then, she's been an integral part of Melba's, and people come from miles just to eat her gumbo.

As of 2019, ten of our forty-five employees are from our days at Wagner's Meat, and we couldn't be more grateful for them.

Her Name Is Melba's ...

SCOTT »

We decided to name the shop Melba's for a number of reasons.

For one, it brought back fond memories for me. My grand-mother lived with a very sweet woman named Ms. Melba in her later years, and my dad and I loved to trade funny stories about growing up with her. Finally, we leaned a little on the reputation of a former shop called Melba's Ice Cream Parlor, which had closed in the 1980s but had been located not far from where our store stood. It was just enough of a kick to give us a little extra recognition when we opened our doors.

Jane was also a big influence on the marketing and development of Melba's. She insisted that we needed to not only serve po-boys; we needed a po-boy that everyone would talk about.

"We need a guarantee, warranty," she said as we hashed out how to make our po-boys popular. "We need to give people as much shrimp as we can and then stand by it."

So I started looking into food costs. I didn't want popcorn shrimp, which were so small that the only thing you could taste was flour. I wanted shrimp you would remember. I finally settled on forty/fifty shrimp, which means you get about forty to fifty shrimp per pound, and then started just spilling them onto the po-boys to see how many we could fit on with a healthy few still falling off.

It turned out that thirty was the magic number, enough to stuff the sauce-sopping french bread loaf that's unique to New Orleans po-boys and still have several shrimps spilling over. From that point forward, we promoted thirty-shrimp po-boys guaranteed! Today, it's our number-one best seller.

... and She Is Anything but Ordinary

SCOTT »

It's almost easier to say what Melba's *isn't* than what it *is*. On paper, she's a world-class food stop with the finest fried chicken and po-boys in the state. In person, she is as eclectic, unique, and warm as the city she was born in.

Come in on any given day and you'll likely hear people singing in line and even whole singing groups sitting at tables and belting out sweet gospel music and classic Motown.

Then there are the artists. Even we are surprised at how many come to Melba's. New Orleans seems to be a magnet for people looking to make a career out of their talents—and we encourage them! From millennials showing up on their bikes with guitar in hand to self-taught street artists looking for a place to hang a few of their works, Melba's thrives on the diverse and many-layered talents of our community. Generations of New Orleans families hang out here, and tourists leave the French Quarter to visit us and experience a place "where the locals eat." Don't be surprised if you find yourself standing in line at the same time as a **Marianite nun** and a **bounce rapper,** both of them just looking for a comfortable place to enjoy a meal; all of them, you included, are Melba's joyful, beating heart, and we welcome all with open arms.

Speaking of unique characters, Melba's is the only place I know with an in-house attorney—not for the business but for the customers. Richard, a friend of ours who has a single practice as a criminal attorney, was looking to drum up some business a while back and asked if he could set up a sign at Melba's. His idea was to drop by for a few hours on Saturdays and offer **free legal advice** 🔍 to whoever needed it.

"Why not?" I said, and so he did.

Week after week Richard came in and set up his homemade sign at one of our booths. Within a month, he had people standing in line to ask him questions. He was getting business, and we were selling sandwiches. It was a match made in Melba's.

Then there's the unordinary setup of our food stop.

Remember that idea I had to split the space into half coffee shop, half laundromat? Well, the laundromat is still here, and it's thriving. When you walk in, the menu and ordering counter are straight ahead, extra tables are on the right, and on your left is an open space with about thirty washing machines and just as many dryers. People drop by to run a couple loads and grab a sandwich while they wait.

It's hard not to remember Melba's. Just like a good gumbo, it sticks with you and keeps you warm long after you leave.

INC. 500 LIST
AND THE FASTEST GROWING
COMPANY IN LOUISIANA

SCOTT »

Our son-in-law **Seth** 🔍 is always impressed when he hears we've hit another record. As an attorney with his own firm, he knows how hard it is to get a profitable business going—offering affordable rates while generating quality product is not an easy thing to do. Entrepreneurs have to wear dozens of hats while also keeping balls in the air, plates spinning, and any other euphemism you can think of that means "insanely busy!"

One day, Seth emailed an application to me for *Inc.* magazine's Fastest Growing Companies in America award. At first I told him I just didn't have time, but as I read through the qualifications, I started thinking, "Hey, we fit these criteria pretty well."

Plus, getting any kind of recognition for good food in New Orleans is an epic battle. I knew for a fact that **Dooky Chase** 🔍, a seventy-year-old establishment that's been voted Best Fried Chicken in New Orleans every year without fail, wasn't even close to selling

120,000 pieces of chicken a month (Melba's 2018 average). We also caught up with the sales of Parkway Bakery—a ninety-year-old French bread bakery—just four years after we opened; and they had an eighty-five-year head start!

I didn't have fifty more years to spend in business before the public considered Melba's a food institution, so we had to find another way.

To challenge the throne of industry titans, you need an army, and I realized that the Inc. award could very well be the key to building that army.

"Congratulations!" the email read. "You have been selected by *Inc.* **Magazine for the Inc. 500 List** 🔍 . You are officially one of our Fastest Growing Companies, ranked #1 in Louisiana and #123 in America."

We couldn't believe it. Even as Jane and I traveled to San Antonio, Texas, and received the award at a beautiful resort with two thousand other attendees and Tony Robbins as the keynote speaker, we were in awe. In our Wagner days, we had been selected as a **top inner-city business** 🔍 in America, and we'd done it again: one little po-boy shop and it was one of the fastest growing companies in America.

Today, Melba's is as credible as the other legacy food institutions in our city, and we've practically become a household name. Wherever we go, people recognize the Melba's name. And not only have they been there, they love it.

❖ ❖ ❖

ANOTHER ROUND WITH THE CABBAGE COOKERS

SCOTT»

For years an old, abandoned house stood across the street from Melba's. Homeless people frequently slept there, and it was in such disrepair that it made the entire neighborhood look seedy.

Then one day I saw someone removing lumber from it, so I walked over to see what was going on.

"You own this place?" I asked him after a quick hello.

"Yup"

"You want to sell it?"

He shook his head. "Talk to the bank. They're repossessing it."

I rubbed my chin for a moment in thought, then asked, "Mind if I paint it?"

"I don't care what you do."

The next day, I asked my painter to get some white paint and do the entire exterior of the house. It looked beautiful; the bright new finish just popped in the otherwise subtle neighborhood. In fact, it was eye-catching. Everyone saw it when they drove by, and in fact, the house was located at an odd little jog in the street that made the driver turn their wheel just a little bit to avoid hitting it.

It was, in other words, the best place in the world for a billboard, and the billboard was "free."

The next morning I called my painter again and said, "We need to paint that house again, but this time in Melba's blue. And we need to do our logo across one entire wall, **'Eat at Melba's.'** 🔍 "

When he was finished, it looked like Andy Warhol had painted it; it nearly punched you in the face through your windshield as you drove by. No one could miss it.

And no one did, particularly the city inspectors. They started sending in complaints almost before the paint was dry. At the same time, local media jumped on the story, asking readers if it was art or crime. I received a certified letter from the city government telling me to remove the sign or face jail time.

Interestingly, the more the painting aggravated city hall, the more popular it became, and the more determined I was to leave it up. The controversy was worth the fine. After months of being on display, they finally got me in for a court hearing. Everyone from the city departments, everyone I'd ever rubbed the wrong way (and there were a few of them on the government payroll), was there. One by one, each department head took a turn at the podium, standing in front of a six-foot-tall projector screen showing the mural, and decried the devastation I'd caused in their wholesome city.

Finally, it was my turn.

I looked around at the room and simply said to the judge, "Your Honor, I recommend you find me innocent, and if guilty, that you impose the smallest fine possible."

Everyone in the room laughed. They knew my cabbage was cooked.

The judge was unimpressed.

"Mr. Wolfe, I do find you liable, and I will impose the maximum fine the law allows."

"And what's that?" I asked.

"Three thousand dollars."

I laughed so hard it brought tears to my eyes. That was it? I couldn't have bought a fraction of the advertising I'd gotten from this whole ordeal for that amount. I could hear a groan ripple through the crowd; they'd waited months to bring me to court, couldn't wait to see me bowed and whimpering under the heavy hand of the law, and I was not only walking out unscathed, I was practically skipping.

I wrote that check then and there and then waited the maximum window of two months before removing the mural. It was the best local advertising campaign I'd ever done.

And by the way, photos of our murals wound up in an exhibit at the Ogden Museum of Southern Art!

Following Our Hearts

JANE »

On the employee side of things at Melba's, I was still fighting for what I knew in my heart was right. To push forth an economic paradigm that takes money from a CEO's pocketbook is a balancing act. I like to think few women can find the energy to muster what it takes to go against the capitalist mindset. On many occasions my husband would say, "Just go out and shop, Jane!" Sometimes I wondered why I was fighting, but then I thought of the eyes of Lois. We had the opportunity to make a difference in the lives of our employees. We had to make a deeper change regarding *our* wages in the retail/service industry, and I told Scott so.

He wouldn't hear it at first.

"For goodness' sake, Jane," he argued. "The employees manage one restaurant! I pay everyone better than what they could get anywhere else."

I let him have his say, but I would not be swayed. Even though we paid well and worked hard to provide a great place to work, Scott's bottom-line mindset was not letting him see past the barrier of worker versus owner. He had the upper hand in the economic relationship, and because he paid more than the federal minimum wage, he was able to sleep at night, believing he was being generous.

But I was having trouble sleeping.

What Scott wasn't keeping in mind was what happened when employees who had been with us for decades were no longer employable. Lois, who had been with us for more than twenty years and cooked the gumbo, red beans, and cabbage, made a difference in our success.

Before our loyal and longtime employees began to question what they had to show after years of dedication, apart from the ability to scrape by from paycheck to paycheck, I wanted to answer that question for them.

The need for business owners to value social impact on the same level as profit and margins is not a new thing, but more than a hundred years after Pope Leo's letter, it is still desperately underrepresented. **Poverty, as Pope Francis expressed, is not inevitable.** But it takes people in business opening their hearts and seeing the exponential impact that caring for their people, employees and customers alike, has on the bottom line to bring that change about.

The value of a business is not static, and the rules and regulations around the distribution of business capital is a minefield to navigate, but I knew what we needed to do.

The business needed to be more economically beneficial to the employees who built it and who kept its doors open, its floors and tables sparkling, and its food as warm, hearty, and wholesome as anything Momma would make. We needed Lois to know she was valued and that she should be compensated for the value she produced.

The business needed to be more economically beneficial to the employees who built it and who kept its doors open, its floors and tables sparkling, and its food as warm, hearty, and wholesome as anything momma would make.

Melba's needed to become a cooperative.

THE POWER OF ENGAGEMENT...

SCOTT»

We rarely realize the impact we have on others.

As young, successful entrepreneurs, we made positive impacts on our customers and the people we worked with, even though we didn't realize it until much later in life. As our customers and employees grew up with us, they shared their gratitude and how much we inspired them, which surprised us to no end. We thought that all we were doing was operating a small business and treating people fairly, just like any company would. But what we were doing meant so much more, and if we'd *known* what we were doing, we would have done it even more.

We never understood that legacy was as valuable as income until our Melba's days. Now, we get cards from former employees we haven't seen in years, telling us how they moved into professional careers and all the things they learned from us working in the grocery stores. Even Wagner's Meat customers, now turned Melba's regulars, tell us how we became an extension of their family, a trusted source and a sanctuary in an otherwise violent and not-so-Big-Easy city.

It wasn't because we were trying to check off some kind of societal outreach box on our business checklist. We did the things we did because we wanted to. Over the past forty years, so many of the community promotions we ran were because we simply saw a need and Jane pushed me to do it. The free-ice-cream-for-As program at Wagner's, for instance, was simply because Jane saw these young children every day who simply needed a little bit of encouragement. The inspirational quotes on the readerboard in front the first Wagner's Meat? That was because Jane felt for all the struggling mothers coming into the grocery who had to weigh buying milk or bread for her family, as they couldn't afford both that week. She wanted them to know that there was hope, that there was still love in this world. And she continues in that vein of love and caring today, whether it's encouraging **early literacy** at the laundromat next to Melba's, providing support to adults working on their GEDs, or giving away **free books to Melba's customers,** Jane pushes all of us to engage the community in ways I never considered.

Caring for the people you work with goes beyond a pat on the back, the occasional raise. It means listening to them—and not just listening but actually *hearing* what they have to say and, if necessary, taking action on it.

I'll never forget the conversation I had with a female employee during Melba's early years. She'd fallen out of favor with the staff because of her poor attitude, which is the fastest way to get booted from our company. Before I took action, however, I took her aside and told her exactly what was going on, that I was surprised at her attitude and was thinking about letting her go. Could she tell me what was going on?

Her response surprised me even further. Her boyfriend had recently broken up with her and kicked her out of the house, leaving her and her three children homeless. She'd been forced to move into a motel that was costing her a full day's pay just to stay, and with little food and the kids left to police themselves, she was constantly on edge.

That simple interest in her wellbeing made her feel like she wasn't invisible. I reminded her that it's always darkest before dawn, and she wasn't the only one at Melba's who'd faced seemingly insurmountable challenges. But just like an iceberg, if you continue to chip, chip, chip away at the issue, eventually it will crack.

I gave her a couple hundred dollars and some extra food to take back to the motel and later helped her find an apartment she could afford. It wasn't the money or the food that helped her adjust, it was the conversation that helped her refocus on her path. Talk, listen with open ears and an open heart, and be genuinely supportive. That's often all it takes to build a team as tight and loyal as they come.

JANE »

When it comes to business, we have to follow our hearts.

When I see government bills to raise the minimum wage being vetoed and people across America walking the streets with posters protesting the decision, I don't want any part of it. The value of a retail or service business relies strongly on the value its people bring to it, and they should be compensated for that, not treated like gig workers who can be cast aside when cheaper labor comes along!

For Lois, the economy had not been kind. She struggled from an early age with the New Orleans school system, but when she began working with us at Wagner's many years ago, she poured herself into her work. Lois has given us the best years of her life, and Melba's would not be the same without her. For all that, she should have something to show for it.

I understand money isn't everything, but some money is better than no money, and we should give what we can.

SCOTT »

Just as I had promised Jane before we opened Melba's, we found a way to offer living wages to our employees. We began by offering a higher base wage than any other fast food, retail, or service location in our neighborhood.

Melba's has a stable workforce. It's not just because of the benefits (even though they do play a big part) but because of how much we value each and every employee. From business cards to featuring pictures of staff and their families at the front counter in big, glamor-shot posters, we empower our team with both responsibility and pride.

When you step back and assess your business by its reach and its employees rather than inventory and equipment, it can be an enlightening and sobering experience. Learning about the people you work with, showing a true interest, can be tough to get in the habit of doing, but if you look for creative ways to show them how much they mean to you, even if it's as simple as asking how things are going at home and how you can help, you will build authentic loyalty and a stable employee base faster than any soulless, half-hearted incentive program ever could. It's not much money to give a little more, and that little bit can actually save you money in ways you may not even realize. Plus, it just makes everyone feel good.

I'm proud of what we've accomplished in New Orleans. It has not been easy. In my younger years, I might have gauged our success by the number of stores we'd opened or the number of employees we managed, but that's no longer my goal. Today, I no longer jump on opportunities simply because I'm afraid of losing them. Now, I see opportunities as something to be explored, and if it doesn't work out, it wasn't meant for me. My mental appetite has slowed down to the rate of my physical one.

I no longer want hundreds of stores. I want time to paint and play with my grandkids. I want to write children's books for them and read it to them at bedtime, and I hope someday they'll read those stories to their own kids and share their memories of a funny old grandpa they knew as Poppy who ran a few groceries *and* America's busiest po-boy shop.

❖ ❖ ❖

... AND SLOWING DOWN TO SEE THE BIGGER PICTURE

JANE »

The week before graduation, a young man asked if I would share with him the secret to success.

He'd asked some other entrepreneurs whom he regarded as successful the same thing, inviting them to join him and a few other Harvard seniors for a casual conversation in Harvard Yard. When the day came, the Yard was filled with inquisitive students, all curious to learn the reason for our success in life.

When my turn came, I could tell he was ready for a long answer, which was why my one-word answer perplexed him.

"Love!" I said.

"That's it?" he asked.

"Yup, that's the reason."

It was the answer I knew in my heart was true.

I was unconditionally loved as a child, I explained. I was never concerned about failure or coming up against the word no. I had every confidence in the world that I would succeed at whatever I put my heart into. Even when Scott and I told my parents that I was pregnant at fifteen years young, the love they showed me was limitless. They were disappointed, and the tears that welled up in their eyes spoke volumes of the dreams they'd had for me, but their love was unwavering. I never felt like less of a daughter to them, and because of that, I faced the world with unparalleled confidence.

When a person is loved, I told the young man, they're not afraid to make mistakes. They automatically have a leg up on the competition because they not only believe in what they're doing, they believe in themselves.

The senior was astonished at the simple but emotional answer.

That talk about success reminded me of that day, so many years ago, when Mr. Roosevelt warned us about the robbery. He was looking out for us. Some forty years after that robbery, my dad told me about another encounter with Mr. Roosevelt. It was back when he still ran Ideal Food Store. He'd just locked up, the day's earnings in a paper bag under his arm, when he saw Mr. Roosevelt across the street, fixing something under his car. Suddenly, the car jack gave way and crashed down on Mr. Roosevelt.

To this day, my dad said, he still has no idea how he garnered the strength to pick up that car.

Love is a powerful thing.

* * *

If Scott didn't have open ears and an open mind, we never would have considered making Melba's a restaurant cooperative. (I compliment his mother for these remarkable qualities.) If I hadn't taken the time to get a higher education, I doubt we would have considered it either, because something we don't often realize about academia is that it forces us to slow down. We can't just live in the weeds. We have to step back and observe the entire landscape too.

It was a challenge sometimes to get Scott to slow down, take a step back, and see the bigger picture. He needed me to remind him about the value of sharing good news and our responsibilities to our neighborhoods beyond simply providing food and jobs. We had a social responsibility as well. So many business people are like Scott, believing that if they are making a profit, everything is good. But it doesn't stop there. Businesses of every size are responsible not just for what's going on in their patch of weeds but also how the actions they take in those weeds is impacting the landscape. They are causing ripples, no matter what they're doing, so are they stepping back, checking themselves to see exactly what impact those ripples are having?

I did not realize how fortunate it was that I had earned a degree in world religion until I saw how thoroughly my learning tied to what I naturally understood of business.

Religion and commerce don't just intersect; they are deeply interwoven. Religion informs so many of our choices. As **Rev. Scotty McLennan** 🔍 at Harvard Business School says, "You really can't do business in the United Arab Emirates without knowing something about Islam, just as you can't really do business in China without knowing anything about Confucianism or in India without knowing anything about Hinduism."

Who but someone with a rich background in world religions could help businesspeople see the greater picture? Who better to sit on a board and advise larger companies who have lost sight of their kaleidoscope of clientele?

For a long time I was conditioned to believe that the poverty surrounding our grocery stores was there because people didn't have the work ethic to get themselves out of their situations. What I discovered was how structures that had been put into place with the intention of alleviating poverty actually contributed to that very mindset. If I had not taken myself out of the weeds and pursued higher education, I never would have noticed these societally limiting economic structures. I never would have discovered that, to change any system, you need to know what makes the system tick.

There were times in **graduate school** that I felt like the smartest person in the room because of what I had learned in our Ninth Ward grocery stores.

I am so thankful for my education and so glad that this perspective allowed me to see what we should have done for our employees a long time ago.

The act of making money is easy. It's like a magic trick. Give someone what they need, and you make a few dollars in the process. It's quite easy to be interesting in the realm of the marketing world too. The hard part is being *interested* and creating a business that has lasting impact, one that people want to keep around and work with because it resonates with them. And it's knowing what resonates—knowing what good news they need to hear, engaging with them and uplifting their spirits, feeding their souls and minds as well as their bellies—that's key.

Businesses can't do this when they stay in the weeds and focus only on profit. They need to see what the ripples of their business touch every day and make sure they're having the impact they want others to see in the world.

Our ripple could be summed up in a ten-cent ice cream cone. We didn't see divisions in our community, and we didn't hold someone's past against them. We believed in character, we supported those who needed it, and in the worst weather, we shared what was good. Our ripple radiated from one of the greatest marketing messages of all time, which we'd also made our own:

Love thy neighbor.

This is why these days we're giving birth to Melba's **cooperative** 🔍 po-boy shop. It was in the class **"God and Money"** 🔍 taught by Professor Harvey Cox where I finally understood that Scott and I needed to share more than we were sharing. We weren't the only ones making our business profitable. People at Melba's put their heart and hard work into making sales climb, and they needed to benefit from it as much as we did.

Businesses must move their eyes from bottom-line thinking and go beyond the letter of the legal minimum law. "Be fruitful and share." These four words can change the world, and today, at Melba's, it is as much a part of our business model as loving thy neighbor.

QR CODES

PAGE 9
"Civil Rights Act"

PAGE 9
"Desire Street"

PAGE 13
"Ideal Food Store"

PAGE 13
"Desire Housing Project"

PAGE 16
"shotgun marriage"

PAGE 17
"Disney World"

PAGE 24

"We were the first ones outside the home"

PAGE 25

"GEDs"

PAGE 26

"robbery"

PAGE 28

"T-Boy was shot and killed by his wife"

PAGE 42

"Positioning"

PAGE 47

"James Carville"

PAGE 48

"You Can't Beat ... Wagner's Meat"

PAGE 49

"readerboard"

PAGE 56

"Ms. Dot"

PAGE 62

"World War II apartment
homes"

PAGE 66

"battle"

PAGE 85

"Times-Picayune"

PAGE 85

"burned at the stake"

PAGE 87

"Hurricane Katrina"

PAGE 89

"St. Rita's Nursing Home"

PAGE 94

"I couldn't process what I was seeing"

PAGE 97

"Wolfman Construction"

PAGE 101

"roofing jobs"

PAGE 110

"Tulane University"

PAGE 111

"grandmother alumni"

PAGE 113

"Harvard Divinity School"

PAGE 115

"twenty-page syllabus"

PAGE 115

"Rerum Novarum"

PAGE 131

"free legal advice"

PAGE 133

"Seth"

PAGE 133

"Dooky Chase"

PAGE 134

"Top inner-city business"

PAGE 134

"*Inc.* Magazine for the Inc. 500 List"

PAGE 136

"Eat at Melba's"

PAGE 138

"Poverty, as Pope Francis expressed, is not inevitable"

PAGE 142

"Free Books to Melba's Customers"

PHOTO JOURNAL

Scott and Jane's GEDs

Wedding day, 1980

Jane and Scott Sr. with Scotty, 1981

Ideal Food Store, Mazant and N. Miro Street, New Orleans, 1978
Jane's mom, Joy, pictured in front

Desire Housing Project, 1956
Courtesy New Orleans Public Library

First market. Desire Street, New Orleans

Wagner's meat counter

9th Ward, New Orleans

Message plastered in New Orleans

Neighborhood Readerboards

Hurricane Katrina business devastation

DEAR WORLD Exhibit
Kennedy School of Government

Harvard Divinity School Graduation, 2015

Editorial spread in *Inc.* magazine, 2016

Celebrating local academic achievement

Engaged entrepreneurship

Melba's laundromat kids zone

America's busiest po-boy shop

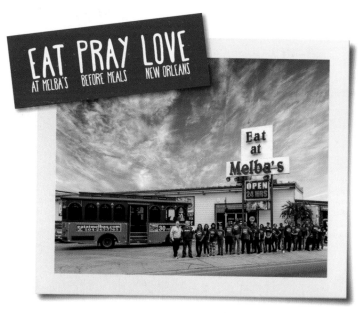

Eat at Melba's, New Orleans